THE WEATHER
Northeast Mississippi — Continued warm and humid through Thursday with thunderstorms likely, mainly during the afternoon and evening hours. Night, upper 60s to low 90s, low low 70s.

Daily Journal

The morning paper, so full of news. It's read all day

Ph: 842-2611   Price 15 Cents   Tupelo, Mississippi, Wednesday Morning, August 17, 1977   Vol. 104 No. 118   5 Green St. East of Hospital

The King Is Dead

Entire Nation Mourns Death Of Tupelo's Own Elvis Presley

Presley is shown during performance earlier this year.

UPI Telephoto

MEMPHIS, Tenn. (UPI) — Elvis Presley, the gyrating king of rock 'n' roll who forever changed the face of music two decades ago, was found slumped "from the Palm" when he Won't Nothin' Act a Hound Dog," died at his adopted homety of at "wrapped heartbeat."

The 42-year old singer — "From the Palm" when he born, took the earth in the mid-1950s — saw fans down on the floor of a bathroom at his Graceland mansion.

He was found there by his road manager Joe Esposito, at 2:30 p.m. Baptist Memphis County Medical Examiner Dr. Jerry Francisco said Presley may have been dead since 8 a.m.

Francisco told newsmen after an autopsy that Presley died of "cardiac arrhythmia," which he described as a severely irregular heartbeat. He said it was brought about by "undetermined causes."

Both Francisco and Dr. George Nichopoulos, Presley's personal physician, said there was "no evidence of any illegal drug use."

Efforts to revive Presley were attempted at Baptist Hospital at 3:30 p.m.

Francisco told at a news conference that "There was no sign cardiovascular disease present. He had a...

Related stories on Page 14

...history of mild hypertension and some coronary artery disease. These two diseases may be enough big for the cardiac arrhythmia. But the precise cause was not determined."

Nichopoulos said Presley was taking medicine for his blood pressure several different kinds, and for colon problem that he had.

basically it was a natural death.

The precise cause of death may never be discovered," he said.

"There certainly were probed drugs being given for the medical condition that was present. There was no evidence of excessive narcotics..."

"I arrived at the Stadium about 3:30 p.m.," said Nichopoulos. "An ambulance was leaving the house. I got over to where he was dead at the time."

"He was lying on the floor on the floor. The people in the house with him were asleep and were not aware that anything [happened] to [his symptoms]."

Michael Presley went to a Justice Monday night.

Continued on Page 14

Carter Names Alabama

ELVIS

ELVIS

TEXT BY
DAVE MARSH

ART DIRECTION BY
BEA FEITLER

SMITHMARK

© 1982 by Straight Arrow Publishers, Inc.

1290 Avenue of the Americas, NY, NY 10104

Introduction by Dave Marsh, © 1992 Duke and Duchess Ventures, Inc.

This edition published in 1997 by

SMITHMARK Publishers

a division of US Media Holdings, Inc.

16 East 32nd Street,

New York, NY 10016

SMITHMARK books are available for bulk purchase

for sales, promotion, and premium use. For details,

write or call the manager of special sales,

SMITHMARK Publishers

16 East 32nd Street

New York, NY l0016

(212) 532-6600

This book is printed under special agreement with

Thunder's Mouth Press

54 Green Street

NY, NY 10013

Printed in the United States of America

ISBN: 0-7651-9495-3

10 9 8 7 6 5 4 3 2 1

ACKNOWLEDGMENTS

The editors wish to acknowledge the following people whose cooperation and help were essential to the creation of this book.

Dave Marsh would like to thank: Barbara Downey and Greil Marcus for their editorial support and advice; Sarah Lazin for the opportunity; Debbie Geller for the consistent assistance; Janelle McComb, Bruce Jackson, Malcolm Leo and Jerry Schilling for their insight and encouragement.

Bea Feitler would especially like to thank Carl Barile, Pat Stuppi, Aileen Natrella and Nicholas Vreeland for their constant support and assistance.

The editors of Rolling Stone Press would like to thank Peggy Allen, who coordinated the photo research for this book; also Jim Nettleton, Linda Perney, Patty Romanowski, Carol Sonenklar, Ron Furmanek and Michael Ochs. We also appreciate the efforts of Times Books editor Patrick Filley, as well as Louis Schauer, Jane Sanderson, Rose Clayton and the many people in Memphis who graciously provided information and assistance.

*E*lvis is the craziest book I've ever written, and in a way, it may be the craziest of all the crazy books ever written about Elvis.

The specifics of that craziness rest in the presumption that the story of Elvis Aaron Presley, son of Tupelo, Mississippi, Memphis, Tennessee, his mother's bosom, rhythm & blues, the old South, and modern America, can be told rationally. It presumes that there is a way to make sense of how one man rose up out of the abjection of Southern poverty, and that if you think about it hard enough, not only the man but his music and his audience and even his detractors will come clean.

Ha, ha, ha. Ha. Ha.

As my only defense, however pathetic it may seem, I'd like to point out the time in which the book was written. In 1981, Elvis was still dead and nobody had yet figured out how to deal with it. Elvis had been in the grave for only four years; the shock of his death still hadn't worn off, and the new religion that seems destined to form around his persona and the best of his works had yet to take shape. Certainly, the strategy of denying that he was even really dead hadn't occurred to anybody—at least, not publicly.

Meantime, Elvis was in need of a defender. In 1981, Albert Goldman had just published his definitive smut, a book whose irrational ridicule of Elvis and his environment, with its pathological loathing of all that was Southern, poor, and working class, whether black or white, and a corrective was essential. And since Goldman is the master of the fact that is not quite a fact, it seemed incumbent upon a defender to bear down on what could be known and to struggle with that tiny body of information to make sense of the improbable story that the full rather than the half truth told.

Adopting this crazy notion had its advantages. For one thing, it threw the text back onto the music, which is the most concrete body of evidence Elvis left us, and the questions it posed and, on rare occasion, answered. For another, it presented a chance to pose my own questions about who Elvis was, where he'd come from, why his story resonated, and to ask them from a material basis—to talk about those questions of class and race that our culture almost never deals with directly, which is part of the reason why Elvis' symbolic enactment of the contradictions they pose resonate so deeply and, it would seem, permanently.

Yet the Elvis that emerged from my contemplation of the music and his social context proved no less chimerical than anybody else's version of how he added up. Maybe this is the doom of any attempt to envision a visionary. But at least there's some good stuff here about what it means to conceive of yourself as a worker while harboring artistic dreams, and about the previously ignored or ridiculed post-Army, pre-"comeback" music. And a platform for these extraordinary photographs. Since I had no role in the art direction or photo selection process (for which Peggy Allen and Sarah Lazin deserve the credit), I've never been at all abashed in saying that this is the most beautiful Elvis book, and nothing has ever come close to eclipsing it.

Crazy as it undeniably is, the original text remains basically undisturbed in this edition. To have begun changing it would have meant creating an essentially new document, not only because I now better realize the nuttiness of my perspective but because so much new Elvis stuff has passed this way in the past decade: books, records and a whole lot more. You didn't have to be an Elvis scholar or a tabloid reader to run into all this noise. If necessary, the ghost of Elvis might come to you. There was, for instance, the hot 1990 night that I stood in the back patio portion of Kalamazoo, Michigan's Club Soda, waiting for the beginning of an anticensorship rock benefit. Looming over the club's backyard was an old brick building, half-a-dozen stories tall. A patron saw me looking that way and said, matter-of-factly, "That's where Elvis lives, you know. On the third floor. That Burger King right across the street is where he eats." Needless to say, Elvis wasn't at home, or at least, all his rooms stayed dark and he never turned up, which is just as well, since if he had he'd probably either have complained about the noise or told us how proud he was that his home state was represented by Tipper Gore's old man.

But this is just background noise. The Elvis story has also been reshaped by more significant forces. For one thing, during a brief golden moment in the eighties, RCA Records actually had a director of A&R, Greg Geller, who knew how to treat its Elvis treasures with respect, how to repackage them creatively and with the highest standards. Around the time of what would have been Elvis' fiftieth birthday, Geller put out what remain the best Elvis albums ever assembled. Only a couple of these—notably the blues album, *Reconsider Baby*, and *The Memphis Record*, the album that collects all the great music he made in Memphis in 1969— are conceptually inspired. Only the box set, *Elvis: A Golden Celebration*, on which the early TV show performances and live appearances are finally officially issued, is particularly bold. The rest—albums such as *The Complete Sun Sessions* and *The Number One Hits*—simply find a devoted and loving Elvis fan creating some order out of his catalog.

Maybe that seems like not much but, amid all the static and bullshit, Geller's undertaking was essential and as each of those records appeared, it pulled your attention back to the one truth that you have to be a fool to deny: The continually compelling power of this music and its ability, at least for the duration of any given track, to make sense of itself, transcending any and all efforts at interpretation. Had Elvis' voice emerged from a burning bush, the sense of "I am that I am" emitted from these records could not be clearer. Geller had the guts and vision to get out of its way, and the result was a triumph.

Of course, that golden moment ended as soon as Geller left RCA's employ. Since then, there have been a couple of interesting discoveries—most notably the release of "My Happiness," the original demo Elvis cut with Marion Keisker, in 1990's *The Great Performances* and the various issues of the so-called Million Dollar Quartet session with Jerry Lee Lewis, Carl Perkins, and momentarily, Johnny Cash—but mainly it's been back to normal, with RCA recycling trivia.

One movie offered much more—not Jim Jarmusch's excessively distanced *Mystery Train*, but Thomas Carboy's 27-minute documentary, *Rock 'n' Roll Disciples*, in which Elvis casts an exceedingly long shadow over fans and impersonators. To have people who organize their sex lives around you, years after your death—now *there's* a definition of cultural triumph, and Carboy, while never denying the strangeness of the situation, never condescends for a instant.

Almost everything that was written by anyone claiming to be related to or conceived by him—was sheer junk. There were a few exceptions, not all happy ones. Jane and Michael Stern's *Elvis World* offered a smirking parallel to Albert Goldman's patronizing sneer. Their vision is of Elvis as a nitwit collectible knickknack figurine. If they were as superior to Elvis Presley as they imagine themselves to be, they'd be ashamed to have produced a volume so filled with hateful condescension.

Charles C. Thompson III and James P. Cole's 1991 *The Death of Elvis* presents an analysis of the Presley autopsy and toxicology report which, despite their Geraldo Rivera connection, rarely strains credibility even if it does miss the big picture. At the very least, *The Death of Elvis* serves the extremely useful purpose of debunking both the gushing nonsense about bone cancer to which too many Elvis fans still cling and the stupidities of the Elvis suicide theory Goldman has recently retailed.

The two best recent interpretations of Elvis are nonfiction works of imagination: Elaine Dundy's 1985 *Elvis and Gladys* and Greil Marcus's 1991 *Dead Elvis*. Dundy's book is a marvel of research—she brings the Presley family tree and in particular its dirt-poor western Mississippi environment brilliantly to life. *Elvis and Gladys* is the most truly Southern account of Elvis Presley's career, obsessed with race to the point of racism, saturated with concepts about family and eugenics that would be bizarre if they didn't have such a long history, but also so loving and respectful of this obscure family's origins and roots that Dundy finally overcomes her own worst ideas.

My fellow Elvis obsessive Greil Marcus has performed the inestimable service of collating a massive amount of post-funeral Elvis material. Marcus seems to share my opinion that Elvis is truly dead and yet cannot die, and his awe at what seems to be taking shape—the formation of an actual religious cult whose final trajectory can't as yet be estimated—animates what might otherwise have been just a storehouse collection. While *Dead Elvis* places too much weight on bohemian artworld responses to Elvis, and doesn't devote enough space to the tabloid culture where he is still most beloved, it's still written with great affection and without any hint of the condescension other middle-class Northern intellectuals have brought to the Presley parable.

And a parable the Elvis Presley story undoubtedly is. Meaning, among other things, that when we go seeking Elvis we most often find ourselves. Which brings me to the one posthumous Elvis phenomenon that genuinely disturbs me. Its basis is a folktale about what Elvis actually thought about African-Americans, which finds expression in a quote for which (in true folk legend fashion) no provenance can be located. "The only thing a nigger is good for is to shine my shoes," Elvis supposedly said.

That he did not say this will forever remain unprovable. Elvis was, after all, a white Mississippian whose poor white family's only social distinction (prior to his own emergence in the recording studio) was the virtue of being not-black. Yet whatever we can *prove*, there is plenty of reason to doubt that Elvis ever said such a thing. In the first place, he knew better—in the South, the *value* of Negroes was all too well established. The fable puts a Yankee racist's words in his mouth. (Which makes me regret that much more this book's one really egregious error, its misreading of Sam Phillips, who was, as Greil Marcus wrote, "one of the great pioneers of racial decency in this century." I apologize for belittling a great man.)

Elvis often said things that meant the opposite of the apocryphal quote. Far more than most of the English rock stars who followed him, he was careful to credit his sources and inspirations in rhythm & blues and gospel music. Justifiably embittered by his being lifted up above them on the basis of skin privilege more than talent (which is an important *part* of the truth) as '50s contemporaries like Little Richard and Chuck Berry have been, even they acknowledge Elvis—not Pat Boone or the Crewcuts or any of the other musical/racial separatists of the period—as the gatekeeper whose work gave them access to the Top 40-defined cultural mainstream. As late as his 1968 TV special, Elvis spoke briefly but eloquently of his reverence for black gospel singers in particular.

Most tellingly, the Million Dollar Quartet session tapes, which catch him completely off guard (none of the musicians knew the tape was running), find Elvis telling a tale about being in Las Vegas and hearing a black singer with Billy Ward's Dominoes—Jackie Wilson, it turns out—who completely outdoes him on "Don't Be Cruel." Elvis never uses the word "nigger" here; he refers to Wilson at first just as a "guy," then, in passing, as "a colored guy." Elvis goes on about Wilson's performance for five minutes, rearranges the song to suit Jackie's style, describes him physically, and details his dancing. He is not uncritical—on the other Elvis numbers he does, the guy "tries too hard" but Elvis readily acknowledges that he's been beaten at his own game. The man who uttered the judgment of black people contained in the fable could never have made any such admission. Not in 1957, and not today.

Yet the fable is held as gospel by some of the finest contemporary black musicians, including Vernon Reid of Living Colour and Public Enemy's Chuck D, who summarizes the whole snit with his line, "Elvis was a hero to most / But he doesn't mean shit to me."

Except it isn't a snit. It's a significant symbolic switch, from James Brown, the most revered soul musician, who boasted of his personal closeness to Elvis, to Chuck D, the most respected leader of the hip-hop movement, who disdains any worth Elvis might possess at all. Part of it has to do with the depths of racism to which America has once again descended and the genuine need for black artists to create and sustain a separatist cultural mythology. Elvis was a figure of integration and that figure must now be destroyed or at least diminished.

The rest is a matter for despair. On a symbolic scale, this claim that Elvis was nothing but a Klansman in blue suede shoes may be the greatest Elvis-related tragedy of all. For if Elvis, as I say at the end of this book, was the sort of indispensable cultural pioneer who made the only kind of map we can trust, what does it mean when pioneers of a later generation have to willfully torch that map?

If Elvis Presley's life story means anything at all, it means speaking to the heart of the human desire for freedom and liberation, from the feet to the hips to the heart to the brain. If it stops meaning that, the failure is ours. And even I'm not crazy enough to think that such a failure will have results any better than a diet of burnt bacon and Demerol.

Now, though, I am stuck with this book's commitment to the facts, and the facts are pretty damn sad. One is that the wholeness of our appreciation of Elvis has reached a presumable end; there are now believers and non-believers, in a permanent stand-off. Another is that I now know that when Lester Bangs said that he guaranteed we would never agree on anything else as we agreed on Elvis, he meant that we would never agree on anything at all. A very troubling third is that Elvis himself—who must have felt even more alone than Eileen Myles asserts every Western person must be—never expected any better. And finally, there's the awful knowledge that Elvis got it exactly right in his last great hit: "We can't go on together with suspicious minds / And we can't build our dreams on suspicious minds."

This book was written in the hope that the kind of dreams the life and work of Elvis Presley represented for my generation will somehow continue to be built. As for myself, while I can think, while I can talk, while I can stand, while I can walk, while I can *dream*, I will never entirely let go of the idea that the facts and the dream will someday join together. Against all the evidence, I *am* still crazy enough to retain that hope and proud to have made a book out of it.

—D.M.
January 1992

"You know how it feels,
You understand,
What it is to be a stranger
In this unfriendly land."
—Bobby Bland,
"Lead Me On"

Among the countless clichés Elvis embodied, "living legend" is the most perfectly realized. There is no "real" Elvis. That man, whoever he may have been, disappeared long ago into the mists of legend.

In part, the real Elvis disappeared because, like Abraham Lincoln, he had a unique ability to personalize his moment in history. We made him the repository of our boldest dreams and our deepest fears. In this way, Elvis functioned as a mirror, revealing more about the observer than the observed. After a while, he himself must have had trouble understanding where he began and we left off. Mostly, though, there is no real Elvis because the unprecedented scope of his achievements and his fame devoured whatever is conventionally understood as "self."

Since his death, our recognition of Presley's importance has expanded. His private habits now come under the intense scrutiny that Elvis successfully eluded for most of his lifetime, even though he was perhaps the most famous man in America during what were some of the most media-mad decades in history. Dozens of books and articles have been written in which lies, assumptions, and half-truths are piled upon revelation, as author after author purports to deliver the real Elvis as we have never seen him before. Of course, each writer maintains that only *his* projection of Elvis is true.

Most of what's been written about Elvis since his death proceeds as if Elvis hadn't entered the realm of mythology the night he recorded "That's All Right," as if he hadn't made himself a permanent home in American lore on the night he first stepped up to the mike on the Dorsey Brothers TV show. In the end, selling the true Elvis is like selling gen-u-ine Babe the Blue Ox steaks.

No one myth is large enough to contain Elvis. There are several, each containing many contradictory features, although they can be boiled down into two contrary versions. One contends that Elvis was a failure. He left Sam Phillips, Memphis and the South, Sun Records and rockabilly—his home and place in the world—for Col. Tom Parker, Nashville, Las Vegas, New York and Hollywood, the Army, RCA Victor, a life of hookers, pills and dissolution. In this version, each step Elvis took was a descent, his career an arc of unrelieved disaster.

The second basic Elvis myth insists that he was a savior. In 1981, with Elvis but four years in the grave, Sam Phillips, one of his discoverers, stood at a podium in Memphis and vowed that Elvis Presley was a modern-day version of Jesus Christ. Phillips was merely adding credibility to the attitude Elvis' hard-core followers have adopted since his death, an attitude summed up in the posthumous slogan ELVIS LOVED YOU. It is as if his fabled love made all the excuses necessary, not only for Presley but for everyone—as if the Elvis story were nothing but transcendence and triumph.

There's something foolish and mean about these extreme attitudes, which I think derives from America's dirtiest secret: that most of us suspect we are unworthy of the greatest freedom we have been granted, the freedom to invent ourselves which Elvis epitomizes.

These myths diminish Elvis by reducing his complexity. Whether propagated by biographers like Albert Goldman or sentimental memoirists like Sam Phillips, such versions of Presley's story insist that his life was simple and easy to understand. In fact, the life of Elvis Presley was an incredible tangle of irreconcilable contradictions. In any case, these reductionist myths are irrelevant. Let us concede the worst: that Elvis was nothing more than a junkie pervert. Let us grant the most outrageous fantasy: that he was a messiah or, anyhow, a saint. So what? You don't need to be a great man to be a great artist. Neither version adds or detracts from his art, and it is Elvis' art that reaches us, his art that will continue to inspire—not save—people for decades to come.

Why are these oversimplified versions of Elvis so widespread and so widely accepted? Because they're needed. Some people want to believe Elvis a failure because admitting the magnitude of his success would make their own shortcomings unbearable. Others want to see Elvis as a king, some kind of savior, because granting him such stature places him outside the common realm, beyond criticism but also beyond emulation. Either way, those who hold these simplistic views are exempt from having to live up to the great challenge lives such as Elvis Presley's present to us: the challenge of seizing the chance to invent ourselves and, in the process, reinvent the world.

Elvis stood up to the challenge, and he serves as a beacon for everyone setting out on the path of self-invention and self-realization. By placing Elvis back within the realm of possibility and granting him a very human stature, one precludes his being either hopelessly corrupt or impossibly virtuous. When Elvis Presley sang "Hound Dog" on "The Steve Allen Show," straining against his tuxedo, not quite a good sport because the defiance never left his eyes—in that moment, Elvis became Everyman as king. So maybe it's appropriate that he went down the way he did, for only by failing himself so blatantly and desperately could Elvis prove that he was fundamentally no better or worse than the least of his fans.

Elvis Presley remains a bundle of contradictions, nonetheless: His roots were in abject poverty, yet he rejected despair, not from blindness but rather as an act of will. He was ambitious to the point of greediness but also truly humble and generous. His naïveté about many things concealed his essential shrewdness about what really mattered; his intense sexuality hid a devoted mama's boy; his devotion to a life of luxurious whims, petty luxury and self-indulgence contrasted sharply with his unshakable, workingman's conviction that music was only a job. Elvis believed in the America described to him in high school—a nation where any man could realize any dream because every man started as an equal to all the rest. This constantly forced him into conflict with the central hypocrisy of American life, the nation's dominance by an elite—especially, its cultural domination by that elite and its Old World values.

Throughout his career, patronizing condescension told him, with a sneer of contempt, that his dream was a lie, not even a fantasy any longer, but a fiction kept around not to embolden men, but to keep them in their places. This is what those highbrow and middle-brow pundits are really saying when they describe Elvis as a rube and a hillbilly, a hick and a mark.

To be worshiped as a king was equally a betrayal of Elvis' passion for democracy. The peril of the king is isolation, after all: There is no one who can look him in the eye, but there is also no one into whose eyes he can frankly stare. In this respect, the king and the slave aren't much different.

There are those who claim that his final acquiescence proves the American dream a nightmare, but they're wrong. What Elvis Presley's story really proves is that all dreams become nightmares unless they're carefully nurtured.

Elvis represents the boundaries of America's capacity for self-invention on one hand and for the creation of communities on the other. His story is the ultimate account of cowboy individualism, for where most American pioneers had to invent only themselves, Elvis had to invent his own frontier as well, before he could begin to work on his self. There is no way one man will ever achieve more, working with himself, by himself, than Elvis Presley did.

Throughout our history, the best and bravest Americans have lit out for the frontier. Few of them survived, and fewer still prospered, unless they were able to find a supportive community in which to integrate their values and discoveries—unless they were able to build something much larger than themselves out on the ultrapersonal frontier.

In the America that produced Elvis Presley, individualism was still possible but the integration of such bold men was not. To join any existing community it was necessary to discard precisely those qualities that encourage a man to cut loose and attempt to find himself. Rather than being greeted as an exemplar, he was shunned as an intruder. Nor was Elvis surrounded by people of a calibre from which such a community could be built. In that sense, it's true that Elvis died, not blameless but friendless. If you're looking for a tragedy, there it is.

ELVIS

> *"Whatever our place it has been visited by the stranger, it will never be new again. It is only the vision that can be new; but that is enough."*
> —*Eudora Welty*

> *"Well, they said that you was high class,*
> *Well that was just a lie."*
> —*"Hound Dog"*

Elvis Aaron Presley was born in Tupelo, Mississippi, in his parents' thirty-by-fifteen-foot shotgun shack, on January 8, 1935. His twin, Jesse Garon, was born dead, and it is said for the rest of his days Elvis was fascinated (and terrified) by the thought that he had possessed (and lost) an exact double, perhaps feeling this was proof that he was special, not just weird.

Vernon and Gladys Presley were typical Mississippians of their generation. True, Vernon, at seventeen, had married a woman four years his senior, but their marriage had already survived two years when Elvis was born, and it would survive twenty-three more. And in every other regard, the Presleys were quite ordinary. Vernon and Gladys came from farming families —when they were married, Vernon was still sharecropping with his father. In 1935, they had moved to town, Vernon driving trucks for a dairy and a wholesale grocery, Gladys working at the Tupelo Garment Company as a sewing-machine operator. Like so many others during the Depression, they were rural people in the process of becoming, if not urbanized, at least estranged from the soil. Elvis grew up a town boy with country legacies: He knew about the land mostly as a legend, but, one might suppose, a legend with power. Yet still, his was the first generation of all his kin to know the city first-hand.

The Presleys were poor, about as poor as white Southerners could be. Vernon did not al-ways find work, and for a time he was put away in Parchman Penitentiary on a bad-check charge; apparently Gladys stopped working steadily after the baby came. From time to time, the Presleys lived on welfare. So the question arises whether Elvis grew up "white trash," a matter of some controversy once he became known outside the South.

"White trash" is a Southern term the meaning of which became distorted when it was carried out of the South. For most Southerners, white trash isn't simply a description of poverty. It's a term with connotations of moral degeneracy, despair, shiftlessness, dirt-eating and incestuousness. More than anything, white trash signifies a family that has moved beyond everyday despair (which is taken for granted as the workingman's lot), a family that has surrendered all of its prospects or cannot even recall a time when it had any. In this regard, the Presleys were certainly not white trash. "His mama worked," said one elderly Tupelo resident by way of refuting the charge. "They *all* worked."

To Northerners and aristocratic Southerners, however, white trash means something more casual and less incriminating—it is a description of low economic condition. But even here the term implies an attitude on the part of those who use it. Calling a family white trash (or hillbilly or cracker) is a statement that the family is barbarous, without culture, capable of making a social contribution only with a strong back. And though many Southerners would disavow this judgment, they couldn't deny it because the structure of Southern society is rooted in such distinctions.

The Presleys probably weren't far from falling into that purgatory beyond despair. Vernon Presley, whom his own son described as "a common laborer," was not an ambitious man. Vernon kept himself employed, even if he had to range as far as Memphis—more than seventy miles distant—to do so, but it was undoubtedly Gladys who pushed him, though whether by ordering him about or simply nagging when he loafed, who knows? Anyone could recognize in Vernon Presley the seeds of dim-wittedness and shiftlessness that so often led a family into the total failure associated with every meaning of white trash.

Somebody in the family dreamed big enough

to give Elvis his sense of possibilities, and this was almost certainly Gladys. She knew, by the time Elvis was born, that her own life would never improve much. And after the move to Memphis she began drinking heavily. Like many another mother, Gladys stockpiled her hopes and transmitted them to her son.

"What was it his mother told him?" Greil Marcus wonders in *Mystery Train*. "That he was just as good as anybody? Or did she whisper, late at night when no one else was there to hear, that her boy could never lose?"

The ambitions Gladys Presley meant to instill in her only child were the ordinary working-class aspirations for better-paying work with some security and perhaps even a pension. Possibly she imagined that Elvis would go to trade school or apprentice out to learn some skilled job. Judging by how closely she nurtured him, walking him to school every day until he was fifteen, Gladys may even have dreamed that Elvis would become a preacher. But she never imagined he would become an entertainer; the very idea of any of her kin being regarded as an artist would have been befuddling. The Presleys worked for a living; they did not

honky-tonk, and if they painted, they painted houses and walls.

Elvis almost certainly had no greater hopes, at least not at first. He loved his daddy's truck; maybe he thought he'd become a mechanic, though he would have preferred some job with less sweat involved. Still, in high school, he majored in shop, the typical public-school preparation for a life spent working with the hands.

Yet somewhere along the way, Elvis began to dream bigger. It's impossible to say just when the thoughts entered his head; he probably never expressed them to anyone, not even his mother (though who knows what *he* whispered to *her* in their late-night chats). It might have started when he won second prize at the Mississippi-Alabama Fair and Dairy Show talent contest for his rendition of "Old Shep." The prize was five dollars and free admission to the amusement rides, but ten-year-old Elvis may have obtained a greater gift: inspiration.

A year or so later, Elvis, wanting a bicycle, settled for a far cheaper guitar; his uncles taught him a few chords. And as he played it, or sang in church, or listened to the radio, he must have known he was capable of more, something that

Gladys and Vernon Presley had been married four years when this family portrait was taken (right); Elvis is two or three. Above: the two-room house in Tupelo where Elvis was born. Overleaf: Elvis as a boy. He had wanted the bike for his birthday but got a guitar instead.

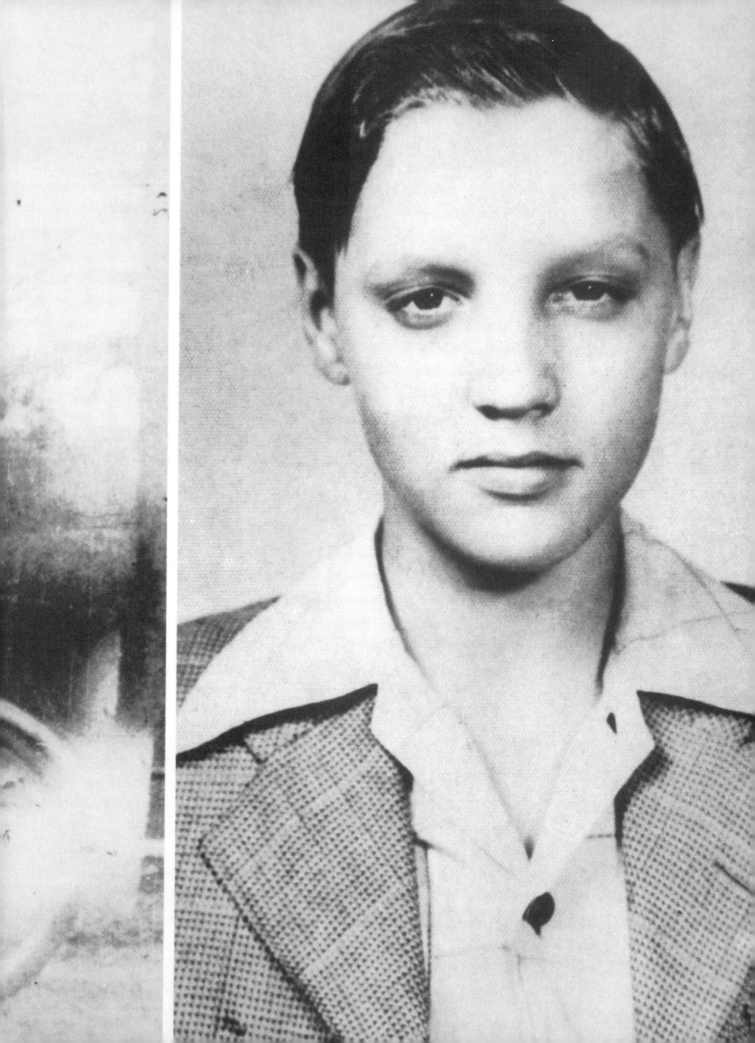

would make up for the slights his precious mama had suffered all these years from "her betters."

For if part of the Southern definition of trash is that it cannot be redeemed by money, it follows that only by means of money may a family's mettle be tested: Poverty is its own excuse —only wealth offers the chance to succeed or fail. So Elvis vowed to get rich, to buy his mama a Cadillac; he told her so out loud, even in front of company. But he never told her how.

Yet he knew; he must have known. He would become a singer—a singer with "a monumental disdain for all those folk who moved easily through a world that had never been easy for him," to quote Marcus again. To put it more exactly, Elvis Presley would become a singer with a *vengeance*.

Music was in the air all around him, and one does not have to romanticize the hard-scrabble South in which Elvis grew up to mean those words literally. He was part of the first generation to grow up with radios, record players and jukeboxes as everyday goods, household appliances. A record player was too expensive for a family like the Presleys but there was always the radio, from which poured a bewildering array of music, from the pop of Frank Sinatra and the Ink Spots to the black gospel blues of Sister Rosetta Tharpe, from the tubercular nasality of Jimmie Rodgers to the sedately holy and occasionally ecstatic harmonizing of the white gospel quartets. In Elvis' head, all these sounds came together as one; he even liked opera, and, judging from his own sense of drama, he learned a thing or two from it.

Blues, country, pop and black gospel he learned from the radio; white gospel he got firsthand. For the Presleys, music began in church, and Elvis later boasted of knowing "practically every religious song that's ever been written."

"When I was four or five," Elvis recalled years later, "all I looked forward to was Sundays, when we all could go to church. This was the only singing training I ever had."

The Presleys attended the First Assembly of God, a Pentecostal church, first in Tupelo and later in Memphis. The Pentecostals are known,

colloquially and contemptuously, as Holy-Rollers, a reference to their wild and ecstatic services and revivals. Theologically ultrafundamentalist, First Assembly of God churches were usually headed by supremely flamboyant preachers, and the congregations were known to speak in tongues, to be taken in fits of ecstatic possession and otherwise engage in dramatic and entertaining acts that testified to their total immersion in the spirit of the Lord. In its theatrics and its fundamentalist beliefs, Pentecostalism is quintessentially a poor man's religion, because it appeals to persons with little sophistication and no other hope.

Elvis clearly learned a good deal of his stagecraft from the preachers of his youth, and it was from them that he learned a good deal of his unorthodoxy, too. For example, Pentecostal ministers are radical in their fundamentalist interpretations of scripture and Elvis eventually devised theories of himself as a prophet and healer.

The Presleys were mostly spectators in their church—at least there are no tales of any of them being dramatically saved. They did not belong to the choir; they sang from their pews (the musical emphasis of the Pentecostal ceremony is on congregational singing, except for certain featured soloists and quartets).

It was quartet singing that made the greatest impression on Elvis. Later, he would say that his musical inspiration was Jake Hess, the great lead singer of the Statesmen Quartet. Throughout his career, Elvis surrounded himself with such gospel groups as the Jordanaires, the Imperials, and J. D. Sumner and the Stamps, combining their voices with his own to form a quartet (as he had done as a schoolboy amateur at all-night gospel sings in Memphis). Usually Elvis and his group sang in the lead, a contrast to the backup-group style of Hess and the Statesmen. On his 1968 TV special, Elvis boiled it down: "Rock & roll is basically just gospel music, or gospel music mixed with rhythm & blues."

Aside from noting that many of the best performances of his later career were of sacred songs, critics have never fully appreciated the importance of Elvis' gospel influences. In part, Presley's gospel involvement seems anomalous

Elvis with his parents outside the Tupelo house. Preceding pages: the front room/bedroom. The house has been restored as a museum, papers on the bed bear news of Elvis' death.

because he looked more like a hoodlum than a choir boy and because the unremitting conservatism of white gospel singing strikes most listeners as the antithesis of Elvis' singing style.

White gospel music *is* conservative; the bulk of it sounds like barbershop hokum to ears tuned to the more antinomian pleasures of rock and R&B. Prior to rock & roll, however, gospel music was the white musical genre most openly and explicitly influenced by black music. This was the result of Pentecostal theology itself being derived in part from black Pentecostal movements of the early 1900s. As with many racial intersections, the Pentecostal music retained black elements long after they were obscured or banished from other portions of the liturgy.

The relationship between black and white gospel singing is further obscured by the drastic changes in black gospel singing since Sam Cooke's recordings with the Soul Stirrers in the early Fifties. Meantime, white quartet styles have changed much less noticeably. Yet a 1954 recording like the Statesmen's "This Ole House" (which became a pop hit for Rosemary Clooney) uses a blues guitar solo that is explicitly derived from black popular music and also quotes from the black spiritual "When the Saints Go Marching In."

One reason white quartet singing sounds so

conservative is that it is based on pre-World War II black gospel styles. After World War II, black gospel focused on vibrant high-tenor lead singers, epitomized by Sam Cooke. There was a corresponding decrease in emphasis on unison and bass singing, which remained central in white quartets. Yet the late Twenties and Thirties recordings of such black sacred groups as the Golden Leaf Quartette, the Birmingham Jubilee Singers and the Four Great Wonders sound very much like the white gospel quartets of Elvis' youth. Not entirely coincidentally, there is a persistence of the "Dr. Watts" and "jubilee" styles of such black groups in Fifties rock & roll. Secularized, these approaches became the doo-wop singing of Sonny Til and the Orioles ("Crying in the Chapel") and Clyde McPhatter's Drifters ("Bells of St. Mary's"). Such groups were also a major influence on Elvis.

Elvis was well aware of the black influence on his favorite groups. "We borrowed the style of our psalm singing from the early Negroes," he later acknowledged. In addition to Sister Rosetta Tharpe's broadcasts, Elvis heard many other black groups at the gospel sings conducted by a Memphis preacher and composer, the Reverend H. W. Brewster. (Later, according to some sources, Elvis met and sang with Bill Johnson's Golden Gate Quartet, one of the premier exponents of jubilee singing, while he was in the Army in West Germany. In any event, Elvis recorded almost all of the songs on the Golden Gates' 1953 Columbia EP on his first gospel album, *His Hand in Mine*.)

Elvis' interest in black gospel music violated no cultural taboo. More than a few whites attended the black gospel shows in Memphis and anyway, many of the most famous sacred songs had been written by a black man, the Reverend Thomas Dorsey, whose classic hymns ("Peace in the Valley," "Take My Hand, Precious Lord") were staples of both black and white groups and churches.

Still, it was fairly unusual for a teenager to be so caught up in gospel singing and to dress as eccentrically as Elvis did. Few other kids at the gospel sings wore pink pegged slacks; the other kids with DA haircuts hardly went to church,

Right: with an early girlfriend in a snapshot taken by his mother, whose shadow falls at lower right. Left: an early high school yearbook picture.

Elvis attended L. C. Humes
High School in Memphis, where
he was a member of ROTC.
Even so, he let his hair grow
long, was a flashy dresser and
hung out on Beale Street, in the
black section of Memphis, the
"home of the blues."

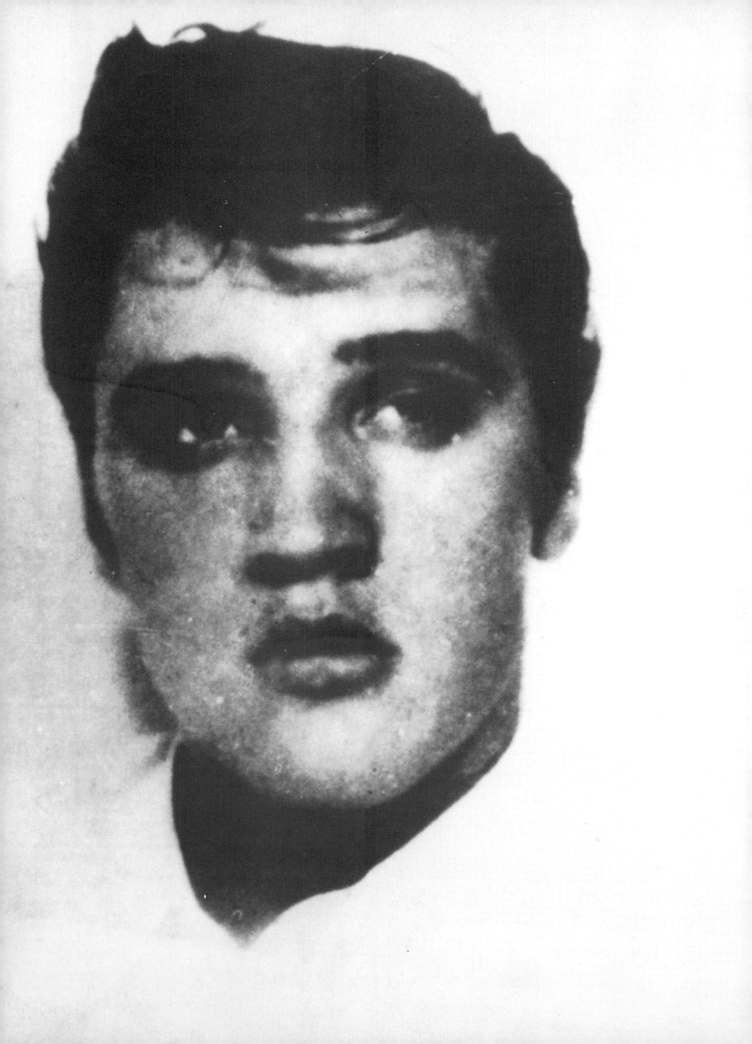

much less dreamed of joining the Blackwoods. This was a reflection of the contradiction that would plague Elvis his whole life: On the one hand, he had a tremendous wish to join the crowd; on the other, an equally powerful need to *show 'em*. He joined the football team in his junior year, but he kept his hair long—a duck's ass in back and a waterfall pompadour in front. He made a splash singing at the talent show; he had a date for the prom. He seized every chance to express himself: football, the gospel sings, sharp clothes and long hair.

Elvis didn't dress strangely to *become* weird; he chose flashy outsider's clothes because he *was* weird. Set down in the poorest part of Memphis at the crucial age of thirteen, he moved from a world of fewer than 10,000 people, where everyone at least knew *about* everyone else, to a world of more than 300,000 that couldn't have cared less about a poor cracker kid—that gaped at his hick idea of what was suave when it paid attention at all. So there he was. Gawky, acned, extraordinarily sheltered even in his poverty; peculiarly shy and polite, hypersensitive to any slight; neither tough nor articulate but inwardly *seething*.

Elvis bought his clothes—outrageously colored and patterned, dramatically cut and flared

Above: the fourth Presley home in Memphis, 462 Alabama Street. Left: Elvis at 18 with an early car, perhaps his father's.

—at Lansky Brothers, down on Beale Street, the border of the toughest, blackest part of Memphis, the storied home of the blues. Lansky's wasn't your typical teenage haberdashery, but then, Elvis wasn't your typical teenager, no matter how much he might sometimes have wished that he were. There wasn't much money to spend on clothes, but Elvis spent all that he had at Lansky's, and certainly, he window-shopped a lot, hung around so much he became familiar in the neighborhood. If B. B. King remembers Elvis from Beale Street, it's probably from seeing him at Lansky's.

Elvis already knew about the blues when he moved to Memphis, but he was too young when he left Tupelo to have fully appreciated the sensuality of the music. In Memphis, the blues were much more available; most white radio stations still played only white records but there was WDIA, the black station that featured such singer/disc jockeys as B. B. King and Rufus Thomas and which was certainly the most exciting and exotic sound in town. There also was Dewey Phillips, on WHBQ, with a blues show on a white station.

Most of all, there was the black section of town, and with the greater anonymity afforded by the larger population, the opportunity to slip around. Elvis (and, according to some accounts, his cousin Billy Smith) prowled the ghetto looking for sex, but he also listened. His taste was forming as he took in the country blues of Arthur "Big Boy" Crudup and Big Bill Broonzy, the more urbane shouting of Roy Brown and Wynonie Harris, the rawer New Orleans music of Lloyd Price and Fats Domino. In time, people would say that Elvis was vulgar; that he had no taste. But those who knew him then say that his taste in rhythm & blues was always superb, and those who have seen the records he collected in the Fifties confirm it.

Elvis liked the blues, but if he had ambitions, they were in the direction of the operatically influenced crooning of Dean Martin or, more practically, joining a gospel quartet. Elvis would never have considered a career as a blues singer; he wasn't honky-tonk enough to want to grow up to be Jimmie Rodgers or Hank Williams, and he wasn't crazy enough to think that a white boy could make a living singing black blues. Even if he could, no white blues singer

was going to make a fortune. No, if the thought ever crossed his mind, he dismissed it and never let it return.

Elvis Presley was not obsessed with blues, but he would soon meet someone who was.

██████████████

"Who is the coolest guy that is what am?"
—*Charlie Rich, "Mohair Sam"*

In June 1953 Elvis graduated from Humes High School and went out to find a job. His first full-time work was in the Precision Tool Company factory, but after only a few weeks he left for a truck-driving and warehouse job with the Crown Electric Company. It was a decent working-class beginning; Elvis made $1.25 an hour—about forty-one dollars a week, take home—not enough to turn any heads, but a substantial sum to the Presley family, which had only recently been removed from the welfare rolls.

It's been said that Elvis found out about Sam Phillips' Memphis Recording Service while driving around town for Crown. Chances are, he was already sufficiently tuned in to the city's music scene to be aware of both the recording service and the record company, Sun, which Phillips ran out of the same studios. Sun cut mostly blues and rhythm & blues records, but it did sometimes record white country-oriented singers and even some gospel sides. The recording service was established as a profitable sideline; its motto was: WE RECORD ANYTHING—ANYTIME—ANYWHERE, $3 One Side, $4 Two Sides. Besides renting equipment for taping weddings and bar mitzvahs, the Memphis Recording Service also made one- or two-sided acetate discs for any amateur musician with a few bucks in his pocket: moony-eyed lovers wanting to impress their honeys, hillbillies off on a binge with an urge for a special memento, young men with big dreams.

Marion Keisker, who usually ran the record-

Elvis in his mid-teens. His taste in rhythm and blues, they later said, was always superb.

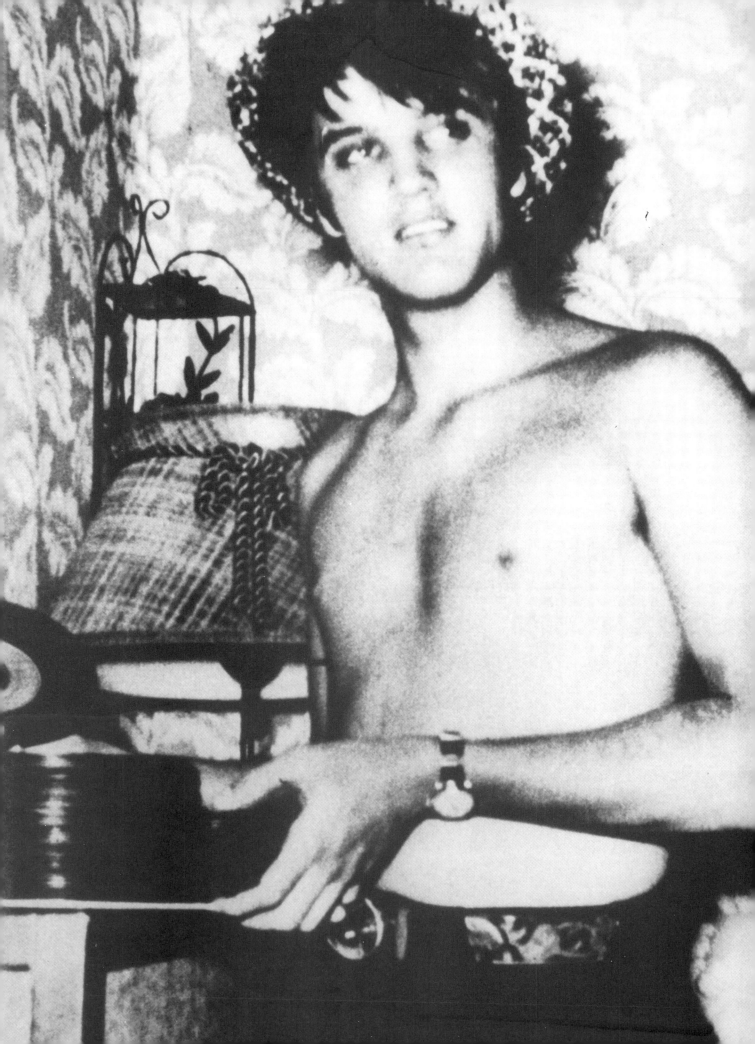

ing service for Phillips, had seen them all. But when Elvis walked through the door that late summer Saturday afternoon, he must have been an odd sight even to her eyes: such a flashy character with such a diffident, courteous, even obsequious manner. The joint was jumping and Elvis had to wait his turn. Perhaps curious about this odd-looking boy, or maybe wanting to set his nerves at ease, Keisker struck up a semblance of conversation with the kid. "What do you sing?" she asked. "I sing all kinds," replied the boy who could never fail. "Who do you sound like?" she wondered. "I don't sound like nobody," answered the boy who would not fit in.

Elvis told Keisker that he was making the record for his mother's birthday, but this seems quite unlikely. Gladys Presley's birthday was in April and, while Keisker has never been able to pinpoint the exact date, she is certain that it was sometime in August or September. Fact is, Elvis wanted to make the record for himself.

Miss Schilling's biology class, with Elvis (upper left).

The way he told it a couple of years later, "I went to Sun, paid my four bucks to the lady because I had a notion to find out what I really sounded like. I had been singing all my life and I was kind of curious."

He must have been not only nervous but awestruck. The Sun studio wasn't much to look at: It was just thirty by eighteen feet, with a bare minimum of equipment. But to Elvis, the microphones and tape decks alone must have made the recording service seem a place of magic.

Elvis wasn't pleased with the record, said it was "terrible . . . sounded like someone beating on a bucket lid." Keisker felt differently, and as he sang she slipped a tape onto the spare machine. This wasn't standard practice at the recording service (why bother?) but Sam Phillips was always saying that if he could find a white man who could sing with the sound and feel of a black man, he could make a billion dollars. Keisker heard something close to what Phillips meant in the way Elvis sang his two Ink Spots numbers ("My Happiness," "That's When Your Heartaches Begin"), something worth preserving for Phillips.

That tape is long gone. So is Elvis' acetate. We are left to wonder what Keisker heard. The

songs came from the repertoire of the Ink Spots, but how does a country boy with an acoustic guitar translate an arrangement created for four urbane voices and an orchestra? We do have Marion Keisker's explanation of what she heard—"what they now call 'soul,' " she told Jerry Hopkins. And history confirms her judgment.

What Elvis made of Keisker's enthusiasm, we can't guess. He didn't know he was auditioning, but he knew that he had impressed her because she took down his address and the phone number of the rabbi who lived downstairs from the Presleys (they had no phone themselves). Maybe he left Sun in a daze; maybe he went away unhappy, thinking that he really did sing miserably, that Keisker wanted to know who he was in order to make fun of his crudity. Or maybe it had all gone just the way he'd dreamed that it would.

Sam Phillips liked the Presley tape but he was not overwhelmed. He has said that he didn't think too much more about it until January 1954, when Elvis again showed up at the recording service. This time, Sam himself was manning the controls. Elvis asked if Keisker had mentioned him; Phillips said he had liked the tape but didn't offer any further encouragement. Elvis paid another four dollars, to record "Casual Love Affair" and a country song, "I'll Never Stand in Your Way." (The source of "Casual Love Affair"—sometimes listed as "Casual Love"—has never been identified, but "I'll Never Stand in Your Way" was a 1941 country hit for Clint Horner, who had written the song, cocredited with Nashville publishing czar Fred Rose.)

This time, apparently, Sam Phillips was more impressed, possibly because he was seeing Elvis firsthand. Or maybe Elvis was just singing better. At any rate, Sam, too, took down Presley's address and phone number. But over the next few weeks, despite Marion Keisker's frequent imploring, Phillips refused to phone Elvis.

Sometime after that second session, Phillips received a demo from Nashville. The song was called "Without You," and Keisker has described it as a "single voice with a single guitar, a simple, lovely ballad." Phillips was prepared to release the tune as it was—he loved not only the song, but the singer. Unfortunately, as often happened, the demo singer was an unknown black kid who just happened to be hanging around the studio. No one knew who he was or where he was now. Phillips was stuck.

Because of the material Elvis had chosen for his recording service demos, Phillips and Keisker thought of him as a ballad singer. So this time Sam agreed to call him. Elvis came running like a shot—so quickly, Phillips would later say, that he'd barely been able to hang up the telephone before Elvis came bursting through the door, eager to start.

Not so fast. Elvis was game, but "Without You" was a difficult song to begin with, and Elvis was soon swamped in its subtleties. He tried the song again and again, but the results weren't simply inadequate, they were terrible, and getting worse.

They took a break and came back to do some more takes. Still, "Without You" remained beyond Elvis—he had met his match. In the wee hours of the morning the session ended. Brutally frustrated, humiliated at the futility of the experience, Elvis exploded, and began pounding the wall with his fists, screaming out his rage against the singer he could not equal. "I hate him!" he cried, over and over. "I hate him! I hate him! I hate him!"

That his career didn't end on the spot can be attributed to that bizarre combination of luck, persistent arrogance, raw talent and gross ambition that sustained Elvis whenever he seemed about to sink. During a break, Phillips asked Elvis what sort of music he *could* sing. That was the luck.

"I can sing anything," Elvis replied, showing his persistence and arrogance.

"Do it," said Sam, and the talent and ambition took over. Elvis began singing everything he knew or imagined doing: blues songs, gospel hymns, honky-tonk hits, old standards and a good deal of the pseudo-sophisticated pop in which Dean Martin then specialized. It poured out of him, a torrent of sound, sometimes just snatches, sometimes whole songs, anything and everything he could think of. And it worked.

Sam Phillips was quite taken with Elvis. "He tried not to show it," Sam told Robert Palmer

in 1978, "but he felt so inferior. He reminded me of a black man in that way. His insecurity was so *markedly* like that of a black person." Elvis probably never exposed himself to another person as he did to Sam Phillips that night.

What he needed most, Elvis said, was a band that could help him work out his ideas. So Phillips put him in touch with Scotty Moore, a twenty-one-year-old guitar player fresh out of the Army. Moore worked in his brother's dry-cleaning plant and played in a country band, the Starlight Wranglers, on the side. Phillips and Moore had spent hours discussing their shared vision of a new musical style that would unite white and black, country, blues and pop elements, and Sam probably wanted to see if Scotty heard in Elvis what he did.

They met at Scotty's house on a Sunday afternoon; Bill Black, a neighbor of Moore's who played bass, was also there. "Elvis came in, he was wearing a pink suit and white shoes and a ducktail. I thought my wife was going to go out the back door," Scotty remembered. "We sat around for a couple of hours, going through a little bit of everything—Marty Robbins, Billy Eckstine, you name it." Moore and Black didn't think Elvis was great, but they liked him well enough to show up at Sun the next day for an audition.

The audition turned into a rehearsal that

Early Sun days: with Sam Phillips (left); with Bill Black and Scotty Moore (above) in their first publicity picture. Preceding pages: 1954 publicity shot (left) and first RCA album cover (right).

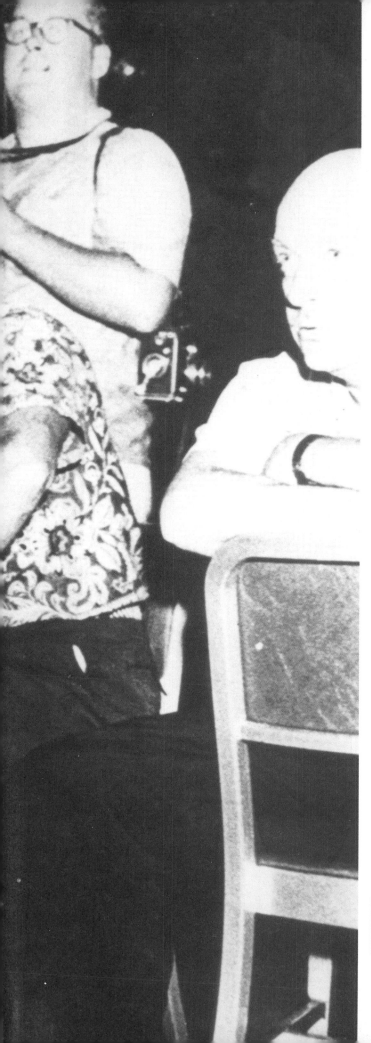

lasted for months, virtually every afternoon and evening after Elvis, Scotty and Bill got off work. As they played together, they grew closer. "You know, we always had a certain bond or understanding, from day one," Scotty said. "We could talk to each other sometimes without saying a word, if that makes any sense at all."

They had only the vaguest idea of what they were looking for; even Phillips, by far the most sophisticated among them, couldn't have given the elusive new sound a name or have clearly identified its structure and elements. What it wasn't was easier to pin down: It wasn't the country-swing R&B Bill Haley had recently begun doing. Haley's music was too stiff and artificial. It wasn't country music; the instrumentation was wrong for that. And it wasn't R&B, because of the instrumentation and because all of the musicians were white. It surely wasn't country blues, even though it was brooding and stark and used a similarly skeletal instrumental setup (Scotty's electric guitar, Bill's

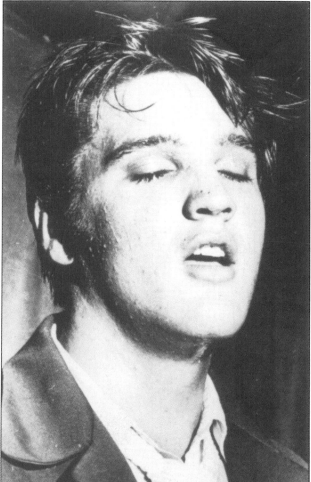

In the first flush of success, Elvis bought his parents a new home on Audubon Drive, a Fifties modern one-story home in the fashionable section of Memphis. It had three bedrooms, including Elvis' pink bedroom (left), a game room, a double carport, and they added a swimming pool soon after moving in.

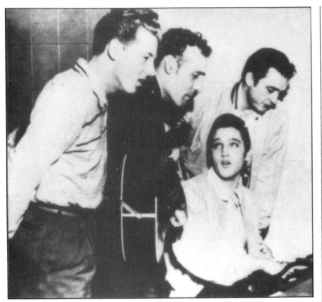

upright bass and Elvis' acoustic guitar, which he often simply banged like a drum). Nor was it straight pop—it was far too syncopated and wild for that, far too willing to use any effect as long as it worked. Lord knows, it wasn't gospel.

It wasn't the first time musicians had deliberately tried crossing such genre barriers. Jimmie Rodgers, the father of country music, had recorded with Louis Armstrong in the early Thirties; country and R&B singers frequently covered one another's material and, since the late Forties, pop singers such as Frankie Laine and Johnnie Ray had made a specialty of creating their hits from tunes originally recorded by country and rhythm & blues artists. (One of Ray's biggest hits, in fact, was a cover of the Prisonaires' "Just Walking in the Rain," a Sun original.) Every Sunday, in strictly segregated churches, black and white Christians sang hymns written by the Reverend Thomas Dorsey and the Reverend Harold Brewster, both black.

But Elvis, Scotty, Bill and Sam were making the first attempt to cross so many barriers simultaneously, merging country, pop, blues, gospel (and even a little operatic drama) into a new and uniquely American style of music.

They surely couldn't have made such a concerted march toward such an unlikely goal at any previous time in history. Elvis, Scotty, Bill and Sam built their music in the recording studio, the first time anyone had ever created a major musical innovation except by working it out in front of a live audience or by laboriously composing it on paper first. Magnetic recording tape had only recently made it possible to do a take of a song, listen to a playback, analyze it, then try another rendition and repeat the process. The old system of direct-to-disc acetate cutting was far too cumbersome and expensive to allow such recording experimentation. (It helped, of course, that Sam Phillips owned not just a record company but also a studio.)

This approach was liberating in two crucial ways—it freed them from the inhibiting effects of audience disapproval while their music developed, and it liberated them from a dependence on tyrannous songwriters since their new style would obliterate any previous version of a song, render it obsolete. This particular group could not have made its breakthrough without that advantage because none of the members was a skilled songwriter. So perhaps their breakthrough was lucky, but then, in the immortal phrase of Branch Rickey, luck is the residue of design. And, in this case, weeks and months of labor.

They hit the new sound while fooling around between takes. Elvis began to sing an Arthur "Big Boy" Crudup country blues, "That's All Right," and Scotty and Bill joined in. From the control booth came Sam's voice, excited. "What are you doing?" They shrugged. "We don't know." "Well, find out . . ." Phillips commanded. "Run through it again. . ."

Every rock writer returns to "That's All Right," as though to the Rosetta stone. It is not the greatest record Presley ever made, and it certainly is not the bluesiest. But it has something else: a beautiful, flowing sense of freedom and release, Elvis' keening voice, so sweet and young, playing off the guitars, Scotty's hungry guitar choogling along neatly until it comes to the break, where it simply struts, definitive, mathematical, a precise statement of everything these young men are all about. Is it art? Is it history? Is it revolution? No one can know, not anymore, unless they were there to hear it before they'd heard any of the other music Elvis made or any of the rock & rollers who followed him. Is it pure magic, a distillation of innocence or just maybe a miracle, a band of cracker boys entering a state of cosmic grace?

A lucky accident at Sun produced the Million Dollar Quartet—Jerry Lee Lewis, Carl Perkins, Johnny Cash with Elvis (above). Opposite: with Charlie Walker, one of the first DJs to play Elvis' records.

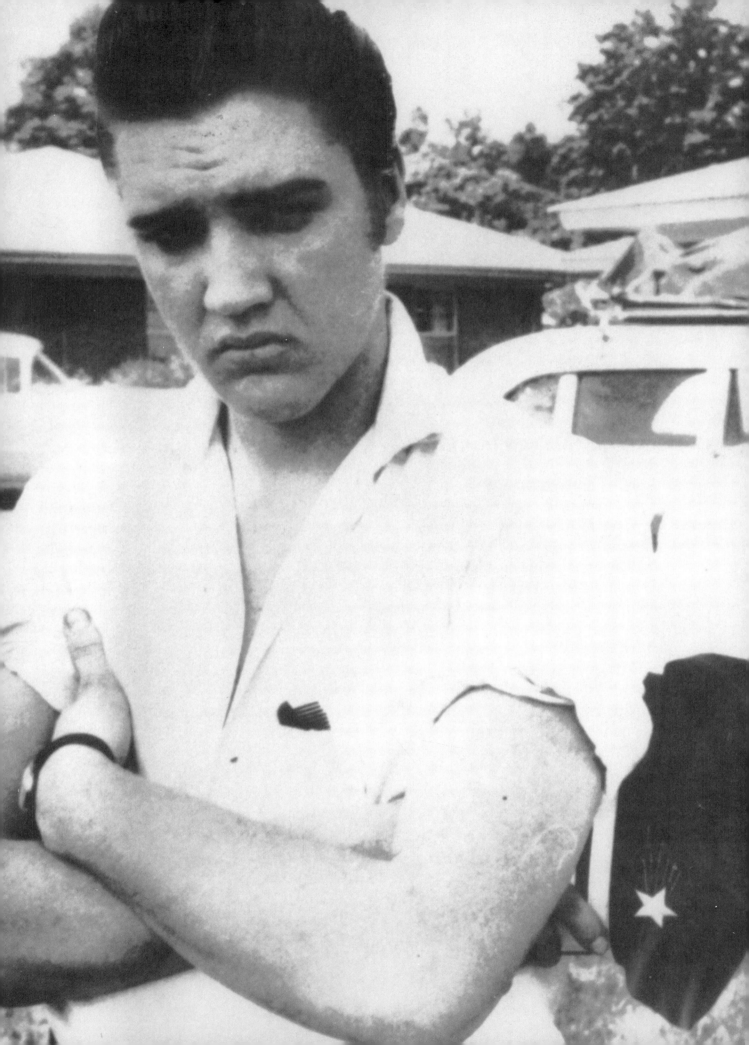

What's most remarkable, given how assiduously pursued this sound had been, is its spontaneity and unselfconsciousness. "That's All Right," like the best of the later Sun material (its B side, "Blue Moon of Kentucky," "Good Rockin' Tonight," "Milkcow Blues Boogie," "You're a Heartbreaker" and, most of all, "Mystery Train"), sounds casual, the kind of music you could hear any day or every day, the kind of sound that has always been familiar but is still surprising. These men are reaching that elusive noise and once they have it in their grasp, they simply toy with it, flipping the thing back and forth among them as if they have been playing with it all their lives.

That is the commonly understood version of what happened up to that great night, July 5, 1954. Sam Phillips now tells a different tale. In his interviews since Elvis' death, he insists that Marion Keisker did not hear Elvis first; that she could not have run the recording service on that day because she

Elvis '56: early days on the road (preceding pages), and at home in Memphis (left). Above: with WHBQ DJ Dewey Phillips.

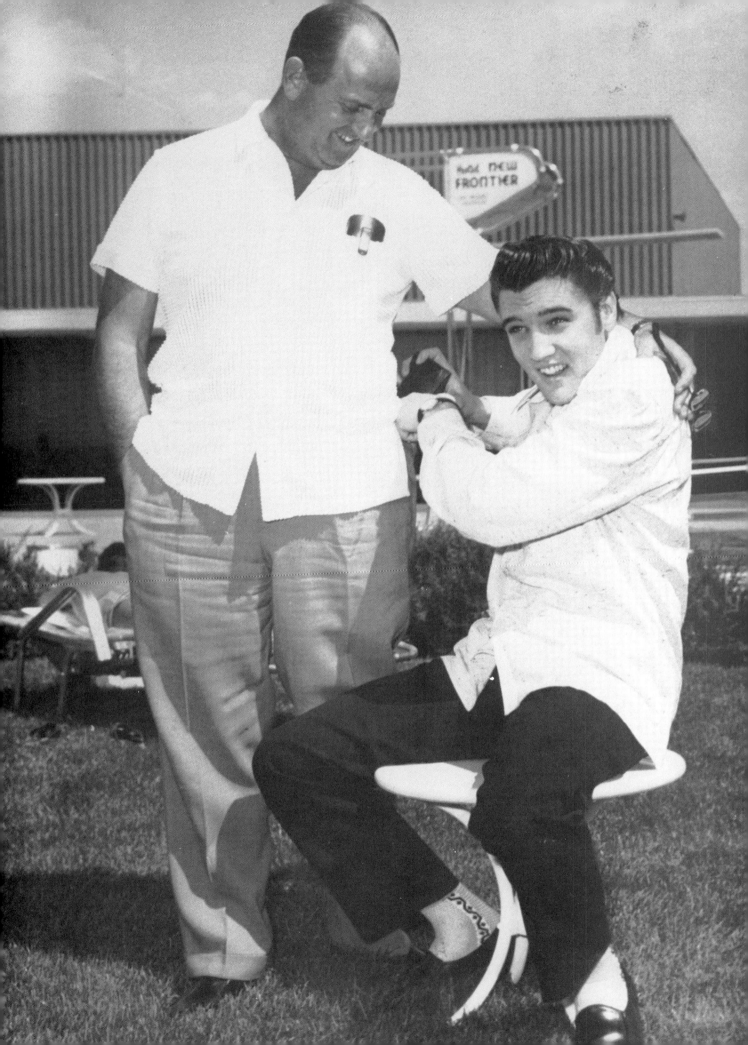

did not know how to thread the tape recorder; that Keisker's story of the "Without You" demo and Elvis' attempt to match it is utterly false, that not only was there no such session, there was no such demo.

Marion Keisker was Sam Phillips' principal assistant at Sun; she'd left a career in Memphis radio, doing her own shows, writing the news, to work there. She certainly knew how to thread a tape machine. As for "Without You," it existed —still does, in the collection of the Memphis fan to whom Keisker gave it. While it's never been widely aired, the music is reportedly so ghostly it's almost freaky; the vocal bears a strong resemblance to Johnny Bragg of the Prisonaires—and to the young Elvis Presley.

This discrepancy would not be especially significant if Sam Phillips hadn't so often been portrayed as the true genius of "That's All Right," and the other Presley Sun recordings; or if the very best Presley historians and critics (Jerry Hopkins, Greil Marcus, Peter Guralnick, Robert Palmer) did not speak of Sam Phillips and his "vision" in terms that border on schoolboy awe, tones that they don't use for Elvis Presley (only for his talent, and perhaps his image).

Sam Phillips was the first representative in Elvis' life of what we may call Certified Cultural Authority, the "real person" who acts as a buffer between Elvis' achievements and his status as an unthinking hillbilly. Phillips is perfect for this role; he is the son of a plantation owner, and his approach to recording has always been purely paternalistic. "...There was a true trust," he told Peter Guralnick in 1979, by way of describing his relationship with Sun's artists. "It was almost like a father-son or big brother-little brother relationship. And I think that adequately describes the feel because . . . good or bad, I was always in charge of my sessions. . . . But at the same time, when I say in charge, it was a type of thing that I made them know I was a part of the total effort. Because they didn't *need* anybody else looking down their nose, they'd had *enough* of that in their life. That would have been the one thing that would have kept them exactly where they were —*nowhere.*"

Elvis bombed in Vegas the first time around. Left: with the Colonel, now a fixture in Elvis' life. Following pages: relaxing back on Audubon Drive.

Sam Phillips may have been as genuinely visionary as he claims. He surely spared his performers as much petty humiliation as possible; one is certain there were no segregated toilets at Sun Records. But Phillips was also a product of his times and his region. In the words above, he insists that he did not reject the blacks and poor whites he recorded, not that he accepted them as equals. And when it came down to treating these performers equally as a matter of dollars and cents, it was a different story: Phillips controlled which songs were recorded; he often took writer's credit where his involvement with composition must have been minimal, and he retained copyright control through his publishing companies. He paid stingy wages and low royalties, a practice which eventually cost Sun all its important stars. But all of this might be said of almost any small-time record entrepreneur. None of it diminishes Phillips' accomplishments in the studio.

However, those accomplishments are much more limited than Phillips and his acolytes suggest. While Phillips seemed to work well with any black performer, regardless of style, he had tremendous difficulty with white musicians who did not know their place—singers like Johnny Cash and Roy Orbison, who came to Sun with their styles already formed or with different tastes than Phillips' own. Phillips claims that his "greatest contribution . . . was to open up an area of freedom within the artist himself, to help him to express what *he* believed

his message to be." But Roy Orbison, for one, left Sun because he wasn't allowed to record his ballads—songs like "Running Scared" and "It's Over," which are some of the greatest rock songs ever waxed. Nor was Elvis allowed to follow the portion of his instinct and talent that led him toward ballad singing.

Elvis did record ballads at Sun: "Blue Moon," "Harbor Lights," "I Love You Because" and "I'll Never Let You Go." But not one of these songs was released by Sun. (RCA issued all but "Harbor Lights" in 1956; "Harbor Lights" was not issued until seventeen years later.) The reason is not that these songs are weaker than Elvis' country blues and rock & roll material of the same period, and it certainly isn't that they are too "unfinished." (Although Phillips says these are early work tapes.) "Blue Moon" is the most frightening performance of Elvis' early, high tenor style, an absolutely eerie masterpiece; it is more exciting and artistically worthwhile than the worst of the releases at Sun—"I Don't Care If the Sun Don't Shine"—and it's at least as polished as the relatively anonymous country tune "I Forgot to Remember to Forget." The fact is that Elvis' vision outstripped that of Sam Phillips from the beginning. It was Phillips who taught Elvis that he was a great natural blues singer, something Elvis might never have realized on his own, and which was a key to everything else Presley would accomplish. But taking Elvis for as much as he was capable of giving was something Sam Phillips could not handle.

Elvis is supposed to have been ruined by his recordings at RCA, made the puppet of a producer's formula. In fact, it was at Sun that he was in the most danger of having his music distorted by a producer. It was Sam Phillips, not Chet Atkins, who recorded Elvis according to a strict and rigid formula. And the fact that Phillips would later apply that formula to performers as deeply talented as Jerry Lee Lewis and Carl Perkins, as marginally gifted as Warren Smith and Billy Lee Riley, and as fundamentally weird as Sonny Burgess and Charlie Feathers, thus creating rockabilly, is not significant here. Phillips had everything to offer such bizarre characters. But Elvis Presley did not want to be a weird rockabilly genius; he wanted to be Elvis Presley.

"Tell the folks back home this is the Promised Land callin', and the poor boy is on the line."
—Chuck Berry,
"Promised Land"

"That's All Right" and its flip side, "Blue Moon of Kentucky," were completed on Monday, July 5, 1954. By Wednesday evening, Dewey Phillips, Sam Phillips' unrelated disc-jockey crony, had "That's All Right" on the air during his "Red Hot and Blue" show on WHBQ. Dewey Phillips was the most important disc jockey in Memphis for white R&B fans and airplay on WHBQ was crucial. Too nervous to stay home and listen, Elvis instructed his parents to tune in and then he split for the movies.

Dewey Phillips liked the Presley record, but he couldn't have expected the response it got: The phones lit up and stayed that way. The station was flooded with requests from listeners wanting to know who the singer was, where this strange noise had come from or simply demanding to hear it again. Phillips kept playing "That's All Right" all night, but his highest priority was to find Elvis for an interview, to establish that he had attended Humes High School—which, in segregated Memphis, was a way of saying that he was white. Many callers had insisted that he must be black.

In light of the controversy that ensued, Elvis might have been better off had the question never been answered. It was no shame to play black music on a white station like WHBQ, and it was not at all strange for white people to listen to such music—otherwise the radio station wouldn't have broadcast the Phillips show. And despite the fact that it is based on a song written by Delta bluesman Arthur Crudup, "That's All Right" doesn't sound like a blues, black *or* white: This was a new form.

There was nothing shameful about appropriating the work of black people, anyway. If Elvis had simply stolen rhythm & blues from Negro

Photographer William Speer took the following portfolio in 1955.

38

culture, as pop-music ignoramuses have for years maintained, there would have been *no reason* for Southern outrage over his new music. (No one complained about Benny Goodman's or Johnnie Ray's expropriations of black styles.) But Elvis did something more daring and dangerous: He not only "sounded like a nigger," he was actively and clearly engaged in race-mixing. The crime of Elvis' rock & roll was that he proved that black and white tendencies could coexist and that the product of their co-existence was not just palatable but thrilling.

Elvis was no revolutionary; he had no interest in becoming a "white Negro," like Norman Mailer and his beatnik pals. Chances are, he went to the movies rather than listen to himself on the radio because he was afraid the reaction would be ridicule. He would have been humiliated and angered that people thought he was black. A poor white Southerner would be hard-pressed to imagine a greater insult.

Sam Phillips, on the other hand, may not have known the extent of the changes white rock & roll would cause, but he certainly knew that the new music would create a fuss. "In fact, he was counting on it." What I was trying to do with white men was to broaden the base," he told Peter Guralnick. "To try to get more radio stations to play this kind of music, to give it more widespread exposure. I knew we had a hard trip for all of us." Scotty Moore and Bill Black also knew that "That's All Right" would cause a ruckus; Moore says his initial reaction to the studio playback was that he would be run out of town.

"That's All Right" didn't hit the record stores for another ten days, and though it climbed to Number Three on the local sales charts by the end of July, Elvis kept on working for Crown Electric. Phillips paid him no advance when he released the record and though Elvis started to do some nightclub dates in the area now that Scotty and Bill had broken up their country act to work with him full-time, he still wasn't making enough money to quit his truck-driving job. And there must have been pressure at home: "I never saw a guitar player worth a damn," Vernon Presley told his son.

Outside of Memphis, "That's All Right" had little impact. *Billboard* gave the disc an encouraging review, and it got a bit of airplay here and there, but Elvis seemed too country for half the disc jockeys and too black for the rest, and without intensive airplay, the record wouldn't sell. Elvis did get a couple of breaks: He received national radio exposure on both "The Grand Ole Opry," the legendary country-music show broadcast by WSM, Nashville, and "The Louisiana Hayride," broadcast by KWKH, Shreveport, Louisiana. Neither show paid much, and the boys had to drive for hours in Scotty's Chevy to get to them, but they were instrumental in getting further attention from the country-music world. (Even though Elvis was not a country performer, there was nowhere else to market a white Southern singer.)

The appearance at the Opry, the older, more established and far more conservative of the shows, was an unqualified disaster. Elvis did both sides of his single, and when he was through, Opry manager Jim Denny told him he should go back to driving trucks. Elvis was reportedly devastated for weeks afterward, but by October he was sufficiently recovered to appear on the "Hayride," where he was a genuine success. He soon became a regular on the weekly broadcasts and signed a one-year contract, later extended to eighteen months.

By January, Elvis was successful enough to sing full-time; he'd quit his job and acquired a manager, Bob Neal, a disc jockey with good connections (among them, the Stars, Inc. agency, which he co-owned with Sam Phillips).

Elvis, Scotty and Bill began to perform live in C&W clubs in a wide arc across the South and Southwest, roaming as far as New Mexico. Like most acts of the time, their show was informal; Elvis often took the stage without any introduction. But when he came out, he dominated, not only singing as well as he did on record but adding that combination of hip-wiggling, pelvis-jiggling, wild-eyed glaring and sensual rocking that would shortly make him a household name. There was bitter talk about him, especially among other performers, many of whom were unable to follow such a dynamic and resourceful act, and many of whom (considering that the act also featured Bill dancing and rolling around with his huge bass fiddle) considered this music beneath their dignity. There was a precedent for this kind of showmanship, but it was not in the country & western nightclubs where they performed; it was in black juke joints and roadhouses. It was an absolutely disreputable display, embarrassing even to hillbilly dignity.

Meantime, there were more records to make. The sessions were never easy because Elvis did not write. Indeed, he and Jerry Lee Lewis are the only important performers in rock & roll history who wrote *none* of their own material. So he wound up cutting tunes that had been hits years before (Keisker says Elvis really wanted to cut *current* hits) or songs that were written by the other performers who were hanging around Sun, or songs that had hit only in the black market. His second release, in September 1954, was a hard-edged version of a 1948 Wynonie Harris R&B hit, "Good Rockin' Tonight," and a country-tinged pop song, "I Don't Care If the Sun Don't Shine." "I Don't Care . . ." is by far the worst song Elvis released at Sun, jumpy and jive, without soul.

"Good Rockin' Tonight" is pure genius, surpassing the first single. Anyone who doubts Elvis' intelligence, particularly his musical intelli-

An exchange with Liberace at the Riviera Hotel in Las Vegas. Following pages: television appearances in New York, 1956.

gence, should listen to "That's All Right," back-to-back with "Good Rockin' Tonight." True, "Good Rockin' Tonight" is a better song, but Elvis' interpretation of it is more sophisticated, more powerful, more *commanding* than the earlier records. He might have lucked into his first triumph, but the second one was earned, obviously the product of craft as much as inspiration.

"Good Rockin' Tonight" also got a nice write-up in *Billboard* but outside Memphis it didn't do as well in airplay or sales. Elvis' third single was released in January 1955, "Milkcow Blues Boogie" and "You're a Heartbreaker," another blues-derived song coupled with a country-oriented flip side. It sold still less and wasn't even reviewed in *Billboard*.

There were probably a number of factors contributing to the declining acceptance of Elvis' records. A good deal of the attention given "That's All Right" was a response to its sheer novelty. And truth to tell, the Presley records were becoming less commercial and accessible, rocking harder. That was their glory but it was also their downfall. Not very many DJs knew what to do with them. This sort of rock & roll was anything but trendy. But the bottom line

was that there was continuing resistance—both to the music and to Elvis—among record men and radio programmers.

The insular Nashville recording establishment soon determined to put a stop to what the Alabama White Citizens Council would call "this animalistic nigger bop." Nashville executives were quite good at this sort of thing; the country-music world was a closed community, more aloof from the record business as a whole than even the blues and R&B worlds. Radio programmers and disc jockeys got the word.

So did *Billboard*. Paul Ackerman, the paper's music editor from the Forties through the Sixties and the man who coined the terms "country & western" and "rhythm & blues" to replace the pejorative "hillbilly" and "race" designations, recounted part of the story in a 1958 article he wrote for *High Fidelity*: "Well-entrenched artists, talent managers and other members of the trade resented him [Elvis] fiercely. One day I had two phone calls from music executives in Nashville, Tennessee. Both demanded that *The Billboard* remove Presley from the best-selling country chart on the ground that—so they said—he was not truly representative of the country field. One of them said bluntly, 'He sings nigger music!' (We didn't take him off.)"

Ackerman resisted the pressure for several reasons. First of all, he was an aficionado of American music who thought that the Presley records were exceptional. Also, he genuinely liked Sam Phillips. Over the years, indeed, Sam and Ackerman would become so close that after the journalist died in 1977 Sam Phillips delivered a eulogy at his funeral, saying, "We could never have made it without his support."

Ackerman's support was also practical. As early as the late Forties, he wrote in *High Fidelity*, *Billboard* began to receive reports of heavy R&B sales in previously white stores; by the early Fifties, the major labels in the North (RCA, Columbia, Decca/Coral, Mercury) were copying a significant number of R&B hits with white artists. "As an interesting corollary," Ackerman noted, "the Negro artists and labels that used to cater primarily to the rhythm & blues market have made a visible effort to become 'pop,' or 'white,' in their musical prod-

Preceding pages: with the Colonel, by now Elvis' manager. Mama (above) in her new home, and with a new hat.

54

uct." Nashville might have to be dragged kicking and screaming into the future, but Ackerman knew that an approach like the one Elvis was using was inevitable in the future of country music, too.

One part of the country establishment, at least, *was* willing to work with the unorthodox new singer. That winter Bob Neal arranged for Elvis to be booked by All Star Attractions, owned by the manager of country star Hank Snow, Col. Thomas A. Parker, a quasi-legendary carny barker and C&W hustler.

In May 1955, Elvis went out on his first major tour, a three-week jaunt headlined by Snow and also featuring Faron Young, Mother Maybelle and the Carter Sisters, the Wilburn Brothers and Slim Whitman (an early Elvis enthusiast).

Elvis' fourth Sun single, "Baby, Let's Play House" and "I'm Left, You're Right, She's Gone" (again, a blues backed by a C&W tune, both jumped up beyond recognition), was issued on April 1, but it was not until late June that it took off. In Jacksonville, Florida, right after the Fourth of July, Elvis, for the first time, had his shirt, jacket and even his shoes ripped off by screaming teenage girls. The sensuality of his stage show, the pure fuck-me splendor of his movements, his athletic grace, began to strike sparks. Passion smoldered; occasionally it burst into flame: Boys became as hostile as their girlfriends became aroused. At least once, Elvis got punched in the face after a show; many other times he was threatened.

"Baby, Let's Play House" was a breakout in Houston, New Orleans, Nashville, Dallas, Richmond, the Carolinas, St. Louis—the areas the tours took him. This is particularly ironic since Elvis' brand of rock & roll was such a pure concoction of the recording studio. Even stranger, at least from the point of view of Presley purists, is that "Baby, Let's Play House," the most successful of his Sun singles, his real commercial breakthrough, is an elaborate plaything, almost a joke, totally self-conscious. The song has its share of true eroticism, but from the beginning, when Elvis stutters "B-b-b-baby," like a man with terminal hiccoughs, to the end, when he repeats the stutter effect just for kicks, "Baby, Let's Play House" is also a parody of lust, an ironic commentary on rock & roll itself. In the

first lines, subtly altered from Arthur Gunter's original, he wrapped his sexiness and his sense of humor together so tightly that nobody will ever unravel them:

Well, you may go to college, you may go to school,
You may have a PINK CADILLAC
But don't you be nobody's fool.
Now, baby, come back, baby, come back,
Come back, baby, come back,
Come back, baby, I wanna play house with you.

This is a performance so sly that it's hard to believe that only a year before Elvis had been pounding the wall at Sun, cursing the anonymous singer whose quality he could not match.

There's also the sense that Elvis is not even using all of his talent, that he refuses to let the job of singing "Baby, Let's Play House" seem as difficult as it really is. This is the essence of what Sam Phillips has termed Elvis' "impudence." Offstage, he may have been humble, addressing all adults as "sir" and "ma'am." But in performance he was already deeply into a wily *noblesse oblige*, a king without a crown.

Or maybe not. Perhaps he was merely frustrated, fed up, eager to get on with his own pink Cadillac. The Presleys had never owned a new car before Elvis became a singer and, car crazy as both Elvis and Vernon were, it's no wonder that a new automobile was one of Elvis' first purchases once he began to make some real money ($200 to $400 a night, split fifty-fifty with Scotty and Bill—that is, 25 percent to each of them, half for Elvis alone—after expenses and 15 percent off the top for Bob Neal). And Elvis didn't get just one car. He got a bunch of them, beginning with a black '51 Lincoln Continental, which he and Scotty and Bill used for touring. When he totaled the Lincoln, he bought a '54 Cadillac and a pink Ford, which he gave to his parents but took back after the Caddy burned up out on the road. He'd have more Cadillacs—he'd have a *pink* Cadillac before the turn of the year.

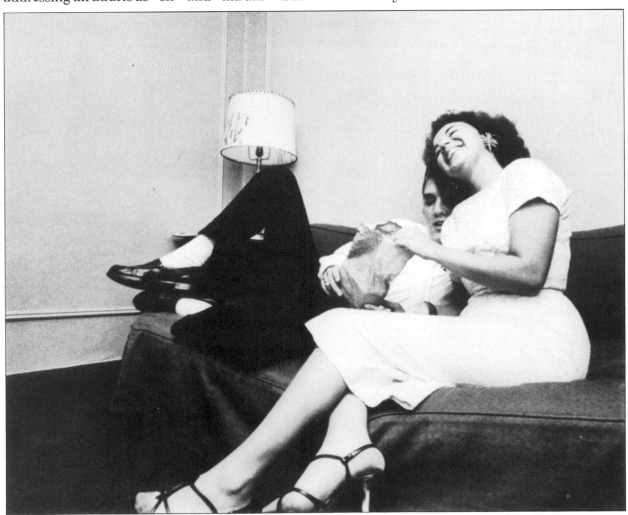

Preceding pages and above: with bodyguards, including Red West, and a new friend in a hotel room on tour.

It may have been obvious to the rest of the music industry that some form of white R&B was going to be the next big thing, that the sound the Cleveland disc jockey Alan Freed called "rock & roll" was on the verge of becoming a major trend. It may even have been clear to shrewd operators that the spearhead of this trend was going to be the Presley kid, although no one could have imagined how big he would get. But Sam Phillips had cold feet.

Some of his fears were perfectly reasonable. First of all, a really big hit could destroy a company the size of Sun, since the label would have to spend enormous sums on pressing and distribution, and there was a good chance that the company's distributors might not pay up unless there was an equally important followup.

Meanwhile, Col. Parker had been edging his way closer to full command of Elvis' career. Parker was telling Bob Neal what to do, when to do it and with whom to do it. With his carny shrewdness, the Colonel understood that the way to Elvis' heart and hip pocket was through his parents. He quickly won over Vernon by appealing to his greed, questioning Sun's competence to adequately promote his son's career. More slowly, he waltzed his way into Gladys' affections, telling her that Sun simply made the boy work too hard. There was no way Elvis was going to defy his parents; if they liked the Colonel, the Colonel was in.

With Parker in, Phillips must have known that sooner or later, he and Sun would be out. There simply wasn't enough money in Sun to make it worthwhile for the Colonel to stay there; the only way his percentage could quickly amount to anything substantial was to negotiate new deals for Elvis. The way Phillips had Elvis locked up left the Colonel very little room to maneuver, except as a concert booker. The live shows created only a trickle of cash unless you had enough clout for national exposure—not of "The Louisiana Hayride" sort but the big time: New York and Hollywood, opportunities beyond the grasp of Sun. Parker was already negotiating Presley out of his commitment to the "Hayride."

Sam and Elvis couldn't have remained together anyway. Phillips despised the bland center of pop culture; Elvis wanted to join it.

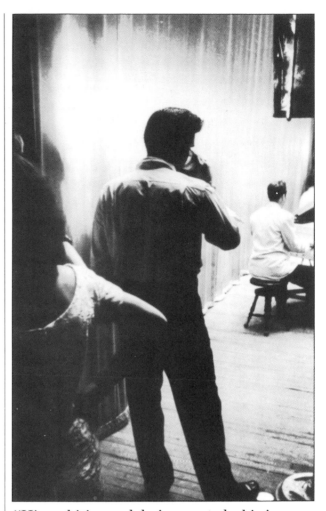

"His ambition and desire was to be big in movies and so forth," Bob Neal said. "From the very first, he had ambition to be nothing in the ordinary but to go all the way." In other words, Elvis did not consider his inability to sing "Without You" a sign that he had failed as a pop singer, but took his later success at one level to imply an ability to win it all.

Phillips, for his part, had newer, more congenial musicians to work with. There was a flood of talent into Sun (and other independent labels) from all over the South—young men, not kids; uneducated but nobody's fools; wild-eyed but aware of their place. These were the rockabillies—rock & roll-singing hillbillies—and they were genuine exotics with bizarre explanations for themselves and their music. Billy Lee Riley swore that Martians had taught him how to bop; Hank Mizell, a Tennessean somehow transported to Chicago, went into a garage and recorded a song called "Jungle Rock," in which he testified that he had observed the very

1956: Presleymania begins in earnest.

beasts of the field beginning to cut up and boogie. Warren Smith summed up the rockabilly world view in the opening lines of his "Ubangi Stomp": "Well, I rocked over Italy, and I rocked over Spain / I rocked in Memphis, *it was all the same.*" There it was: the world as a hillbilly's jungle-boogie dream.

These were the men who made Sun a legend, of whom publicist Bill Williams would say, "All of 'em were totally nuts. They were all free spirits, they were all uniques. I think every one of 'em must have come in on the midnight train from nowhere. I mean, it was like they came from outer space."

These were also the people described by W. J. Cash in *The Mind of the South*: ". . . he is the child man, the primitive stuff of humanity lies very close to the surface in him . . . he likes naively to play, to expand his ego, his senses, his emotions . . . he will accept what pleases him and reject what does not, and . . . in general, he will prefer the extravagant, the flashing and the brightly colored—in a word, he displays the whole catalogue of qualities we mean by romanticism and hedonism." This was, in sum, a typical poor white Southerner who had gone out on the biggest spree of his life and refused to come home, trying to extend Saturday night into a week-long activity.

The leader of the pack was Sam Phillips himself. "Sam's crazy," Jerry Lee Lewis, the grandest rockabilly of them all, said in pure admiration. "Nutty as a fox squirrel. He's just like me, he ain't got no sense." Phillips understood these men, and he knew how to nurture them. Sam had, in fact, been raised with a patrician Southerner's sense that taking care of this sort of person was part of his responsibility. In years to come, he would speak of them as "family," as "boys," as "children," as "little brothers," and he would be right. These men were far more malleable than Elvis, and a couple of them— Jerry Lee in particular—were damned near as talented.

The true archetype of the rockabilly was Carl Perkins, a lean, hungry-eyed Tennessean, reserved and modest in private, but a musical visionary who had worked out a synthesis of his region's music before he heard Elvis. He liked to do John Lee Hooker songs Bill Monroe-style, "blues with a country beat." He came to

Phillips and they recorded the definitive rockabilly sides "Blue Suede Shoes," "Matchbox," "Boppin' the Blues" and the anthemic "Dixie Fried":

*Well, on the outskirts of town, there's a little
    night spot.
Dan dropped in about five o'clock,
Pulled off his coat, said, 'The night is short'
Reached in his pocket and he flashed a quart.
He hollered, 'Rave on, children, I'm with ya
Rave on, cats,' he cried.
'It's almost dawn and the cops are gone
Let's all get Dixie Fried.'*

Perkins doesn't let Dan off the hook: The cops return, and he ends up in the slammer, bemoaning his decision to become Dixie Fried. And this is the rockabilly story in essence: **Men broke through for a moment, were bedazzled and dumbfounded by their freedom and simply retreated**, only a little more aware than when they began. "Give me one hand loose and I'll be satisfied," sang Charlie Feathers, a model rockabilly.

Well, Elvis Presley was no rockabilly. He fought, finger by finger, until he had finally cut *both* hands loose and was set free—as free as anyone in the annals of mankind or fiction. For in truth, Elvis was not the typical Southerner. Cash also described Elvis' type: "Always it was possible for the strong, craving lads who still thrust up from the old sturdy root-stock to make their way out and on." Elvis was no happy cracker, no complacent hillbilly, no white trash. He was a pioneer and, like a trail blazer, he simply lit out for the territory the minute he was given an opening.

Elvis spelled out *his* vision—beholden to no one, with both hands free—in his final Sun single, "Mystery Train." It is a true and total prophecy of where he found himself in the next year; it is the most exciting music he recorded at Sun, and maybe ever. And, most of all, it is a massive gesture of defiance and arrogance— a young man's assertion of his will, not just against record producers and public opinion, but against the world at large.

In both the Carter Family's "Worried Man Blues" (on which the lyric is based) and in Little Junior Parker's original "Mystery Train," this mysterious train escapes with something pre-

cious: a man's life, or his lover, or both. Elvis changes the old story. This train has taken his baby, he says, "but it never will again." And then, he goes a step further:

Train, train comin' down, down the line,
Train, train comin' dow-own the line,
Well, it's bringing *my baby*
'Cause she's mine, all mine . . .

Parker had sung some of the same lines, but wearily, as if the struggle had reduced him. Like the young conqueror that he was, Elvis sang these words as if there had never been any doubt.

Throughout 1955 Col. Tom Parker shopped Elvis around the New York labels. Though he was not yet officially Presley's manager —largely because Elvis wasn't yet twenty-one—Parker was already making every important career decision for him. And the time to move had come.

In August Elvis toured the South, one of the first tours as a star: Miami, Jacksonville, New Orleans.

Three labels were seriously interested in signing Elvis: Columbia and RCA—the two giants of the record industry—and Atlantic, an independent label run by two sons of a Turkish diplomat and a former *Billboard* reporter. CBS offered $15,000 but Sam Phillips insisted that $20,000 was his minimum price. So Mitch Miller, the singalong leader who then ran Columbia's A&R (artist and repertoire) department, passed, vowing angrily that no performer was worth that much money. (Miller banned rock & roll from Columbia altogether, to that label's eventual woe.)

RCA was the least interested of the three bidders. Columbia and Atlantic wanted Elvis because he could help establish them in Nashville; RCA was already a strong presence there. But Steve Sholes, RCA's Nashville vice-president, thought Elvis was talented and he sensed that he was a harbinger of the C&W future (especially given the guidance of the shrewd Parker, with whom Sholes had worked when the Colonel managed Eddy Arnold and Hank Snow, both RCA artists).

Atlantic's bid complicated the picture. Basically, Atlantic represented in New York what Sun did in Memphis: Ahmet and Nesuhi Ertegun and Jerry Wexler were shrewd entrepreneurs who had a genuine feeling for rhythm & blues, which they also recognized in Presley. Elvis would give Atlantic a Nashville beachhead, and the Erteguns and Wexler knew how to exploit his teenage rock & roll appeal better than anyone else. (Far more than Sun, Atlantic had cashed in on the awakening taste for R&B among white kids, with the label's recordings of Big Joe Turner, the Coasters, the Drifters, and the Clovers, among others.)

Somehow, Ahmet Ertegun came up with $25,000 cash, which was fine with Phillips. But Atlantic wasn't the alternative Parker needed. After paying so much cash for Elvis, the label would have little money left for record promotion, and Atlantic had absolutely no clout in movies or television, areas in which Elvis and the Colonel were already deeply interested.

There were other reasons Parker needed RCA. He knew the company because he had once managed Arnold and Snow, two of its most important country acts. RCA was a place where a strong manager could virtually dictate the company's priorities. Just as important, RCA had experience and connections in TV and the movies.

Steve Sholes convinced RCA to bid $25,000 for Elvis, but only at the risk of his job. (He later said that his New York bosses wanted him to guarantee that the company would earn back its investment within a year.) Somehow, though—and this has never been explained—Phillips' price had gone up. Maybe Sam had decided that Elvis had been undervalued or that he could get more by sweating it out. Or maybe the additional money was necessary as part of some scam only the Colonel fully understood. (It's even conceivable, judging from what came next, that Parker was taking a commission from Phillips on the sale, representing both ends against the middle.)

Parker's only connections for capital were in the music industry. There are only two sources of large sums of money in the record business: the labels themselves and music publishers, who collect a fee every time a copyrighted tune is recorded or played. It was common for publishers to act as the industry's bankers, so Parker went to Hill and Range, an important country publishing house run by two German immigrants, Julian and Jean Aberbach. The

Aberbachs agreed to pay Phillips $15,000 (a small fortune at the time) for Hi-Lo Music, the Phillips-owned company that had published the original material Elvis had recorded at Sun. They also agreed to set up two publishing companies for Elvis—Elvis Presley Music and Gladys Music. As administrators, the Aberbachs would effectively control Elvis' publishing interests. (This became especially significant four years after Presley's death, when it was discovered that he was never registered with the performing rights society, BMI, to collect fees owed to him for songs on which he had writer's credit, an omission that cost Elvis hundreds of thousands—if not millions—of dollars.)

When it was announced in November 1955, the deal to purchase Elvis' contract and previously created master recordings from Sun was presented as an outright buy-out by RCA—$35,000 to Phillips and Sun, $5,000 in royalty money to Elvis. Little or no mention was made of Hill and Range's involvement. This may have been because Elvis' association with Hill and Range borders on the inexplicable. Elvis was not a songwriter although his interpretations were often so radical that he could quite legitimately claim arranger credit. (That he would also eventually take credit for songs he did *not* rearrange is beside the point.)

Indeed, a music publishing company was the last thing Elvis needed. As a purely interpretive artist, he was utterly at the mercy of his material and while in the short term Elvis was not prevented from recording material that had previously been published elsewhere, in the long run he was limited to songwriters with a relationship to Hill and Range and its subsidiaries. Initially, he was relatively unaffected because he was so much hotter than anyone else around. Many good rhythm & blues writers found it more profitable to split the publishing rights with Hill and Range and get Elvis to cut their songs than to have anybody else record them and retain all of the rights.

In terms of immediate consequences, the deal was brilliant—for the Colonel. He and Elvis were on the biggest record label in America, and they had cost that label enough money (perhaps a hundred times as much as was normal for an unknown) to insure that, at the least, their

initial recordings would be heavily promoted not only in C&W markets but as mainstream pop records as well. (In the end, RCA also successfully promoted Elvis' pre-Army recordings as rhythm & blues records, with the result that he had more Number One R&B hits than such black performers as Little Richard and Chuck Berry.) RCA rereleased all of the Sun singles before the beginning of the new year and, since Sun was still selling off its old stock, in effect, Elvis had the resources of both companies at his command.

That left only Sam Phillips out of the picture. Later, he would insist, "I haven't regretted selling his contract because I figured then, and still think, that you can't figure an artist's life for more than six months in advance." Phillips also thought that he had in Carl Perkins a talent that was at least a match for Presley's. So Sam Phillips had found his white man with black rhythm and feel, but he did not have a billion dollars: He had $35,000.

No matter. He sank some of Sun's profits into a new Memphis business called Holiday Inn. The payoff was about the same.

"Touring is the roughest part,"
Elvis said. Here, relaxing in
Louisiana. Following pages:
the big New Orleans concert,
where they opened up the stage
to fit an audience in the round.

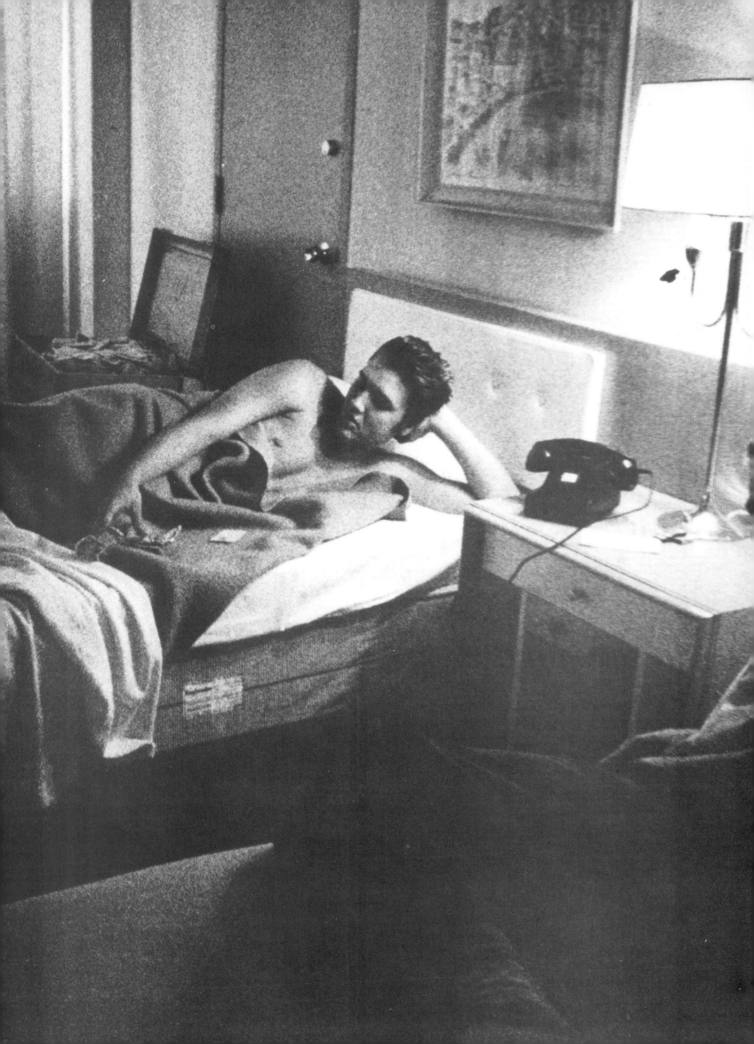

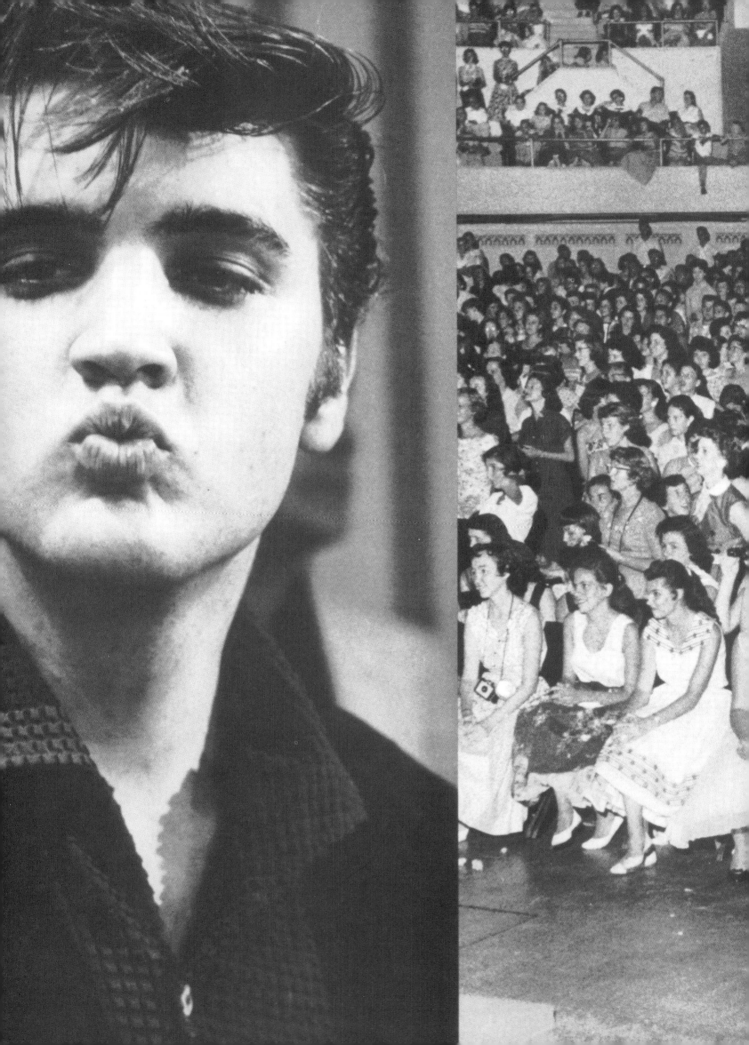

Elvis must have been elated in his new surroundings. He could not have missed the feeling that he had finally made it, escaped anonymity. This was the legitimate big time and if the surroundings were somewhat shabby (RCA's Nashville studio wasn't much more sophisticated than Sun's), the presence of such name musicians as the Jordanaires, Chet Atkins and Floyd Cramer more than compensated.

Elvis now had a little money, some fame and a shot at getting more of both. He had at last been able to move his parents into a decent house, even if he was still on tour so much of the time that he was hardly familiar with his new home. (Symptomatically, Elvis continued to live at home—in fact, it would be three more years before he lived apart from his father, and then only because his mother had died and Vernon had remarried and moved out.) If the rewards weren't yet great, if the grind was exhausting, still, as 1955 drew to a close, he had three songs simultaneously on the national country charts.

Elvis' first recording session for RCA took place in Nashville on January 10 and 11, 1956, only two days after he turned twenty-one. The sessions, produced by Steve Sholes with the assistance of Nashville guitar great Chet Atkins, featured some additions to the basic Sun band: Floyd Cramer on piano with the Jordanaires vocal trio, Atkins on second guitar and D. J. Fontana—now fully integrated into the stage show—on drums. Five songs were completed during the two days, not exceptionally prolific by that era's standards. Three of those five tracks were original songs, including the first single, "Heartbreak Hotel," its B side, "I Was the One" and a ballad, "I'm Counting on You." The other tracks were covers of R&B hits: Ray Charles' "I Got a Woman," from the year before, and "Money Honey," the Drifters' 1953 classic.

Except for the piano and the Jordanaires, "Heartbreak Hotel" and the two R&B covers are obvious attempts to replicate the Sun sound: thus, the overemphasis on echo, which nearly ruins "Heartbreak Hotel," and the lengthy Scotty Moore solos in all of them. Still, Elvis' reading of these songs is nothing to shrug off.

"Money Honey" is brilliant, owing much to Clyde McPhatter's original, but "I Got a Woman" is simply the best performance of the session, a pure, hard blues with a belted-out, swing-style conclusion. Elvis is, in fact, much closer to mid-Fifties R&B styles in these songs than on any of the Sun numbers. For the first time he could really be said to sound "black."

The two other original songs, "I Was the One" and "I'm Counting on You," are more problematic. Elvis completely commits himself to both, but this only renders them more dispiriting—neither song deserves commitment. Elvis could perhaps bring himself to sing these songs wholeheartedly because he was at last singing ballads, which is where he'd always believed his pop-music future was. But, magician that he was, there was very little he could do with this sort of material.

This is the essence of Elvis' problem: "I Was the One" and "I'm Counting on You" are typical of the pop material he would be asked to work with for the next decade. With his acute sense of his own future, it's surprising that he didn't rebel. He may have believed that these songs were merely accidents, or he may actually have considered himself capable of redeeming *any* piece of garbage he was offered. Or maybe he just didn't know how to say no. Musically, Elvis lacked suspicion.

What he should have realized was that he was now entering enemy territory. He had been given fair warning when Jim Denny of the Opry had told him to go back to truck driving the year before. Denny had been speaking for the entire Nashville establishment and, as it turned out, for most of the entrenched business interests of the music industry. Elvis was now in the hands of the very Nashville establishment which had earlier run him out of town: Col. Parker used to book his acts using the phone in the Grand Ole Opry's lobby, and RCA was the most Establishment record label in town. These people represented interests that were threatened by Elvis' success, but they weren't above making money off him. He'd have his hits, make his money. What he would not have was dignity, because the people with whom he would now be working held him and his boogiefied hillbilly routine in contempt.

The popular-music industry of the mid-Fifties

pop music. So Elvis was assigned songs by the worst Hill and Range hacks. Don Robertson, the author of "I'm Counting on You," should never have been given another Presley assignment. Instead, he was assigned to write dozens. To be fair, there weren't many places for Elvis to turn for new songs. He couldn't make a career of R&B covers without being reduced to the level of Pat Boone. This is one thing that mitigated against continuing the Sun approach (and it must be recalled that the original material Elvis recorded at Sun wasn't much better than the worst of what he got at RCA). So Elvis was simply suspended between the Colonel's deals and his own inability to write. When he was given good material (as he often would be, thanks to such writers as Jerry Leiber and Mike Stoller, Otis Blackwell and, a bit later, Doc Pomus and Mort Shuman), he was great. Given mediocre songs, he would transcend their limitations time and again. Given bad songs, he would still plow through.

There was little reason for Elvis to be given anything but the best material—"Heartbreak Hotel," released two weeks after it was recorded, immediately jumped on the *Billboard* charts and rocketed into the Top Forty within a month. Elvis was the hottest singer on the charts, and any songwriter should have been ecstatic at the possibility of having him cut one of their numbers. But this wasn't true, and it wouldn't be even after Elvis (with "I Want You, I Need You, I Love You" and "Love Me Tender") had established himself as a great ballad singer.

The Tin Pan Alley songwriting tradition was imbued with notions of Broadway "class" to which rock & roll in general, and Elvis in particular, were anathema. Tin Pan Alley composers and publishing houses proclaimed his success a fraud, the result of deceit and the disintegrating cultural and moral standards of America (which really meant, the rise of an indigenous American musical style over the European heritage of Tin Pan Alley). They disapproved of *Elvis*—not just of what he sang but of what he represented, not because he was working class (Frank Sinatra was working class) but

was oriented to songwriters, not performers. A hit performance was valuable because it increased the worth of a song by inspiring dozens of other versions, generating wealth for the composer, lyricist and publisher (but nothing extra for the original performer). In the rock & roll era, records would slowly smash this hegemony. For the time being, it might be possible for middle-of-the-road acts like the Crew Cuts and Pat Boone to have hits with cover versions of black songs. But it was only a matter of time before records would be made by black rock & roll performers whose styles were literally inimitable: Little Richard, Chuck Berry, Sam Cooke.

Unfortunately, in January 1956, the music business was still in transition, and Elvis, while providing much of the impetus for the eventual triumph of the performer over the publisher, was trapped nonetheless. The result was malignant neglect and artistic sabotage. Helpless because he couldn't write, Elvis was hamstrung by the unnecessary Hill and Range deal, which linked him to the most conservative forces in

Above: the end of a Southern tour. Following pages: publicity picture with puppy (left); and celebrating Elvis Presley Day (right) with an outdoor concert at the annual fair in Tupelo, where Elvis won his first contest—and five dollars—for singing "Old Shep" in 1945.

because he had no class: He was a Southern hick, and he should have been obliged to keep with his own. Race-mixing, again, only this time the charges came from the North.

Had the Tin Pan Alley publishers and writers been open to Elvis, it wouldn't have made much difference. The price of getting to him was allowing your song to be published by one of his Hill and Range-controlled companies. Anyone with an exclusive agreement with another publisher was automatically barred from having an original number recorded by Elvis. Under these circumstances, it's little wonder that no established pop songwriter provided Elvis with material—although well-known R&B writers often would, since Presley was an open door to the otherwise restricted pop charts. Thus, while Elvis continued to have very good rock and blues material, his pop songs and ballads were mostly treacle. In the end, even after Hill and Range's measly $15,000 had been recouped a hundred times over, the publisher kept Elvis tightly reined.

Elvis rarely disputed his material; he never refused to sing the lackluster tunes he was given even though, behind the scenes, he indicated his contempt for the worst of them. But, mostly, he just didn't rebel.

And no wonder. Consider Elvis in January 1956. He was twenty-one years old, the product of the poorest part of the poorest and most insular part of the nation. He was a spoiled only child who had never been asked to make difficult choices. He was a romantic, given to extremes of politeness and good conduct, not only for his mother's sake but because he truly believed in civics-textbook virtue, in good intentions and the fundamental benevolence and generosity of his betters.

This Elvis had no role models. Other pop singers were not rebelling against the system and the few rebels he did know were country-music honky-tonkers in the Hank Williams mold, clearly destined for self-destruction, their rebellion taking the most trivial shapes: womanizing, drunkenness, drug addiction. This Elvis was inclined to believe what he was told, and each of the hacks who fed him undoubtedly had some marginal composing credit—a Dean Martin B side or a Perry Como LP track—which allowed Elvis to think he was working with big-time boys rather than bozos.

Further weighing against the possibility of rebellion was Elvis' idea of what was "practical." This reflected an instinctive knowledge that it was better not to challenge one's superiors directly, that the liberties that had been granted could easily be taken away. Elvis regarded pop music as a job—"I became a singer because I didn't want to sweat"—and he certainly did not want to lose it.

Then, too, there was Elvis' uncommon mixture of arrogance and humility—if he were bold enough to imagine that he could convert any trashy song into something palatable, he was also humble enough to suspect that he might just deserve nothing better than these tepid little tunes. There can be no doubt, of course, that Elvis understood perfectly well the mediocrity of the songs he was asked to sing. But Elvis did look at music as a job; his primary goal was always money. In that respect, even the worst material was wildly successful; people bought the hell out of it.

They bought it because he was extraordinarily good and because what he did was so liber-

After late 1956, Elvis would never again be so accessible to photographers or to the public. These pages: a brief respite at home.

ating. It was precisely "Heartbreak Hotel" and the other hits Elvis recorded in 1956 ("Don't Be Cruel," "Hound Dog," "I Want You, I Need You, I Love You") that were responsible for inciting what we now recognize as the rock & roll audience into self-awareness for the first time. It is foolish to contend that Elvis was artistically less powerful once he left Sam Phillips' tutelage, because he demonstrated so pragmatically that he was so much *more* powerful.

However, it is true that Elvis' post-Sun music was as "fundamentally silly" as ultrapurist Peter Guralnick argues. This is so for two reasons: First, the material with which Elvis was saddled was fundamentally silly stuff—as silly as "I Don't Care If the Sun Don't Shine." Second, and probably more important, Elvis had developed distancing mechanisms against the potentially crazy reactions of his fans—hostile males and swooning females alike.

That is, Elvis had become a *professional*, and though the concept of professionalism may be anathema to aesthetes, to a man who's trying to learn how to make a living in a world altogether unfamiliar to him, it is an essential quality. And Elvis had not acquired his professionalism any too soon.

I t wasn't his records that ultimately made Elvis Presley a household dream and nightmare; it was those wild-eyed TV performances of his records, sheer, paralyzing intensity brought straight into comfortable homes.

Consider American popular culture in the moments just after 8:00 P.M. on January 28, 1956, as represented (quite accurately) by "The Dorsey Brothers Stage Show." The theme music is a large, bland wad of strings and brass without discernible rhythmic accent. The male entertainers are decked out in tuxedos; suits and ties constitute casual wear except in the odd comedy skit. The only women are skimpily clad dancers. Everyone is white; no one speaks with an accent (except, perhaps, in an ethnic comedy sketch). The atmosphere is polished, sophisticated, slick, easy—nothing is difficult or challenging because there's nothing at stake. Everyone has a role to play, entertainer and

Boxing with perennial sparring partner Red West.

audience, assigned at birth and kept for life.

Enter Elvis, the living antithesis of this culture. Not unkempt but unruly, fresh, arrogant, surly, raw and powerful, his lip curling, hips shaking, knees swiveling. The music is streamlined and defined, his small band louder than the Dorseys' huge orchestra. Elvis snaps into "Heartbreak Hotel." He owns the song and the crowd immediately; the audience is stunned. This isn't so much an "act" as an exposé of the emptiness not only of most entertainment but of most *lives*. In the process of watching him, lives are changed.

Yet the reaction wasn't national convulsion. "Heartbreak Hotel" came out the week Elvis' first Dorsey show aired and, though the song soon topped the national pop and country charts—even got to Number Five in R&B— TV wasn't decisive in its success. The Dorsey show wasn't highly rated; Elvis had been booked because he might boost its ratings. Elvis had been spectacularly successful with his live show in the South and Southwest, radio programmers were becoming more open to rock &

roll with each passing week and he now had a record with the promotional clout of RCA behind it from the day of release. All these factors contributed to Elvis' national breakout.

All this while the band toured ceaselessly, flying into New York to do the TV appearances and to make an occasional record date. Elvis, Scotty, Bill and D. J. Fontana were selling out the honky-tonks and the arenas in the South and Southwest, making an occasional foray into the Middle West but basically avoiding the big cities. It was the country circuit they played. But Parker had bigger ideas.

On April 23, they began what was meant to be a two-week headline engagement at the Frontier Hotel in Las Vegas. It was undiluted disaster. The crowd came to gawk and glare at the hillbilly freak. It sat on its hands, a middle-aged, middle-class wad that wanted nothing more threatening or challenging than a little diversion from its losses at the tables. After the first few days, Presley's name dropped to second on the bill, below comedian Shecky Greene. Before the start of the second week, the Frontier agreed to tear up Elvis' $8500-per-week contract.

The Vegas dates did have one benefit. While watching a lounge act, Freddie Bell and the Bellboys, Elvis and the band heard a trumped-up version of Big Mama Thornton's 1953 R&B hit, "Hound Dog," an arrangement so wild and preposterously stagy that they immediately added it to their own stage show, where it became a sensation.

It was Elvis' performance of "Hound Dog" the second time he appeared on "The Milton Berle Show" that created outrage in papers and pulpits across the land. "Hound Dog" itself, although written as an exercise in black vernacular by a pair of hustling white leftists from Hollywood, Jerry Leiber and Mike Stoller, was greeted as the worst kind of hillbilly barbarism. That is, "You ain't nothin' but a hound dog / Cryin' all the time" was regarded as culturally retarded by a nation that only months before had found "How much is that doggie in the window / The one with the waggily tail" perfectly acceptable.

At right, with early steady Barbara Hearn and stuffed animals. Overleaf: a day off in downtown Memphis.

The biggest outcry was against the way Elvis moved. "Elvis the Pelvis" became an epithet on the lips of the nation's adults, moving Elvis to a rare public expression of bitterness (in a *TV Guide* interview): "It's one of the most childish expressions I ever heard, comin' from an adult." TV critics used Presley's TV performances to argue their case against the decadence and boorishness of the medium; the ordinarily sober John Crosby of the *New York Herald Tribune* called Elvis "unspeakably untalented and vulgar," just short of true obscenity. It was an opinion seconded, often in stronger terms, by preachers, critics and educators across the land.

Elvis claimed not to understand the furor. "I don't see that any type of music would have any bad influence on people," he said, less ingenuously than many suspected. "I can't figure it out . . . I mean, how would rock & roll music make anybody rebel against their parents?" It certainly had not estranged him from his beloved mama, and if rock & roll was all right for Gladys (who was not about to look down upon anything that brought her darling boy such acclaim), it was beyond question in Elvis' eyes.

That was not good enough for the arbiters of taste and morals. Which is amazing, nothing less, considering the context in which Elvis appeared. It would be difficult to imagine anything much more vulgar than Milton Berle himself, with his tit jokes and transvestism, all of it expressed with a smarmy smile and a one-of-the-guys poke in the ribs. And the June Taylor Dancers, featured performers on the Dorsey and Jackie Gleason shows, shook their butts, more sedately but then again, more scantily clad. These things were not "vulgar" because in this sense, the charge of vulgarity was actually code for complaints that Elvis disrupted the order of things. He made the connection between dancing and sex all too obvious, he broke down barriers between the performer and his audience: The studio seats were supposed to be filled with those who would laugh and clap when they were told, but Elvis' teenage fans screamed right through his songs.

Hardly a single critic had any idea of the musical base from which Elvis was working. What the uproar really revealed was the vast Amer-

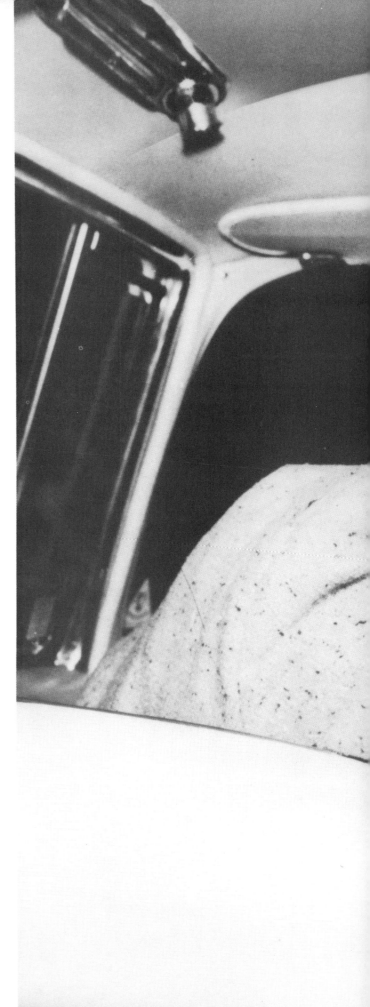

Barbara Hearn on a "Date with Elvis" for a fan magazine.

ican ignorance of its own culture. No critic pointed out the importance of Elvis' synthesis and fusion of various American popular music styles, because it was considered inconceivable that such purely American products could be worthwhile. Few were willing to acknowledge that Elvis' dancing itself had cultural antecedents; those who did merely used the facts to point out how uncivilized Americans remained. The notion that Elvis was in fact the most vital cultural phenomenon of the postwar era would have been greeted with laughter and derision.

There were those, of course, who responded intensely to Elvis' music, but they were mostly teenagers, and though he was spelling out possibilities as yet unfathomed to millions of adolescents, none could rise in his defense: Not even the most silver-tongued teenager could have explained the alchemy of Elvis to an unconvinced adult. You either saw it or you didn't. It split the country.

All this caught the eye of Steve Allen, then hosting a Sunday night variety show. If he outlives Norman Cousins, Allen may yet come to be regarded as this century's preeminent embodiment of the patronizing middlebrow. Allen was a pianist and sometime lyricist (he cowrote "Picnic," a long-forgotten but then voguish movie theme), and he hated the emergent rock & roll; he would later be reduced to reading aloud the lyrics to "Be-Bop-a-Lula." Allen seized the opportunity to present Elvis as a chance to hype his own ratings while putting the young hillbilly in his place.

Elvis appeared on July 1, 1956. The program began with Allen walking onstage dressed in a tux, short hair slicked back, horn-rimmed glasses set firmly on his smirking mug, wringing his hands in gleeful anticipation. "Well, you know, a couple of weeks ago on 'The Milton Berle Show,' our next guest, Elvis Presley, received a great deal of attention—which some people seemed to interpret one way and some viewers interpreted another," Allen said, his silly smirk growing larger. "Naturally, it's our intention to do nothing but a good show. [A bark from offstage; Allen laughs nervously.] We want to do a show the whole family can watch

Elvis rented out a Memphis amusement park on occasion for his friends. Here, with special girl Anita Wood.

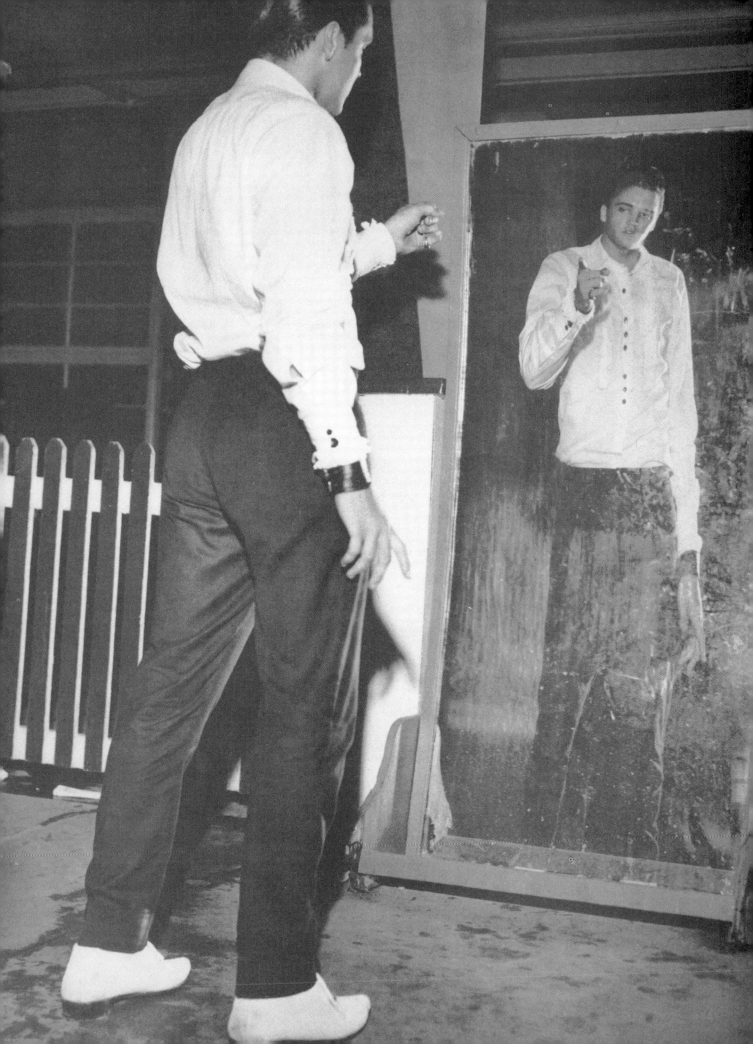

and enjoy and *we always do*. And tonight we are presenting Elvis Presley in his [snicker], what you might call his first comeback. And so it gives me great pleasure to introduce, the new Elvis Presley."

Elvis stood there, decked out in a tux (and blue suede shoes, no less). Elvis beat Allen in the first round, singing a knockout version of "I Want You, I Need You, I Love You," his new single and a fairly conventional ballad that was entirely credible in this getup. Allen then opened a curtain, revealing Elvis' band—and a basset hound perched on a stool, wearing a top hat and a bow tie, to which Elvis was supposed to sing "Hound Dog." He did, and he prevailed yet again, proving himself not only a good sport but an exceptionally intense and witty performer. Only those who gazed long into Presley's eyes could have seen how angry and humiliated he felt.

It got worse, in a comedy skit that featured Allen, Elvis, Imogene Coca and Andy Griffith as what was supposed to be taken as a "typical" hillbilly entertainment troupe devoted to hayseed jokes and the hustling of unmarketable products to the rubes. The jokes were not even up to Allen's usual pallidly "urbane" standards. Each of them was lame, flat but vicious, a pitiless exhibition of Allen's commitment to proving a point: that Elvis and the hillbilly culture he symbolized had *no place* in American life. Twenty-five years later, this skit is virtually incomprehensible except as this sort of basic attack on what Elvis was taken to represent, which was not only the South but lack of "sophistication."

Nor was Allen's intention missed—not by everyone. In *Newsweek*, John Lardner devoted an entire column to Elvis' appearance on the program. Though it was written with Lardner's familial sarcasm, the column ("Devitalizing Elvis") amounts to a defense of Presley. "Steve Allen . . . made a public attempt to neutralize, calm or de-twitch Elvis Presley, the lively singer," Lardner wrote. "Allen did this, one assumes, in what he personally considers the best interests of civilization. For him, it was logical. Civilization today is sharply divided into two schools which cannot stand the sight of each other. One school, Allen's, is torpid or dormant in style; it believes in underplaying, or underbidding, or waiting 'em out. The other, Presley's, is committed to the strategy of open defiance, of confusing 'em, of yelling 'em down. The hips and the Adam's apple, this school believes, must be quicker than the eye.

"Allen's ethics were questionable from the start," Lardner concluded. "He fouled Presley, a fair-minded judge would say, by dressing him like a corpse, in white tie and tails." The corpse, in the long run, would be the bourgeois emptiness Allen epitomized. But for now the humiliation was Elvis'.

He bore up well. Elvis cringed, but he never quit; he proved that he really was a trouper. As a result, Allen's contempt and condescending attitude backfired. Elvis became bigger than ever after this appearance. "The Ed Sullivan Show," which had earlier spurned Col. Parker's overtures, now offered Elvis the then-astounding price of $50,000 for three appearances. By the time the first show aired, on September 9, Elvis had become such a cause célèbre that Sullivan earned an 82.6 percent share of the viewing audience, an estimated 54 million people. (Steve Allen was off the air that night, replaced by a British movie, the network version of a flag of truce.)

Sullivan himself had been almost as derisive of Elvis' ability as Allen. Sullivan wasn't the host on the first Presley-led program—he was ill, so Charles Laughton filled in. But Ed was there when Elvis came back on October 28 and again the following January. By then, everyone but Sullivan and Elvis had forgotten Ed's original snub.

As a result, that final appearance became complicated. As penance for attacking Elvis, the Colonel insisted that Sullivan publicly apologize—which Sullivan did, saying, "I wanted to say to Elvis Presley and the country that this is a real decent, fine boy." But Sullivan and the CBS censors had already contradicted themselves, declaring that for this night, Elvis' "suggestive movements" made it imperative that he be shown only from the waist up. Elvis made a mockery of the censorship, swiveling wildly, bumping and grinding with everything from his elbows to his eyebrows, using his shoulders as a metaphoric pelvis, and grinning wildly at the undiminished screams.

Like every other insult, this one only enhanced Presley's notoriety. Still, the from-the-waist-up edict, like the rest of Elvis' experiences in TV, essentially signified that Elvis Presley remained an outsider, a barbarian welcome to the media moguls but not the culture barons, and then only for his novelty value—and whatever wealth he could generate.

"Elvis, the very definition of rock-and-roll for its vociferous defenders and detractors, became ...[a pioneer] of the unalienated youth movie. You couldn't blame Elvis. In those days, everyone kept speculating about what would happen to punks like him when the rock-and-roll fad was over."

—*Ellen Willis*

Beginning in March 1956 the Colonel placed ads in the trade papers, announcing THE NEW SINGING RAGE!!! ELVIS PRESLEY and designed to draw attention to Elvis for possible movie roles. Within a month, Hal Wallis, a Hollywood veteran who had produced everything from the accidental art film *Casablanca* to a string of Jerry Lewis–Dean Martin quickies, contacted Parker and suggested that Elvis make a screen test at Paramount. When Presley flew to Los Angeles a few weeks later, he made the test. Chances are, he wouldn't have had to be very good to be offered a shot at films. As it was, Wallis came through with the proverbial three-picture deal.

It was not an exceptionally shrewd bargain on the Colonel's part. Wallis offered Elvis an escalating salary of $100,000 for the first film, $150,000 for the second, $200,000 for the third. It did not provide for a percentage of the net or gross (although his other film deals would). Nor did the Colonel seem to shop around for other

possibilities. Perhaps he wanted to nail down something firm in Hollywood right away. Or maybe he was simply on the lookout, as always, for a fast buck. In any event, about the best that could be said for the deal with Wallis and Paramount was that it was nonexclusive. Elvis made two of his first four films with other studios.

It's impossible to discern how good an actor Elvis could have been. Certainly, Pauline Kael's claim that he was always "terrible" is ridiculous. Elvis had some smidgen of talent, but since it was never developed, we can only guess at what might have been. True, his first screen appearance, in *Love Me Tender*, was disastrously mediocre, but the three other pictures he made before his induction into the Army, in March 1958, showed great improvement.

Elvis made those first four films in a little over eighteen months, a pace that didn't allow for the creation of decent properties, much less time for a raw beginner to acquire any craft. Elvis turned down—or was rejected for—far better roles than those he accepted: playing opposite Burt Lancaster in *The Rainmaker*, and the Tony Curtis role in *The Defiant Ones*, parts in *Thunder Road*, *In Cold Blood* and, later, *A Star Is Born*.

The poster announces a benefit concert in a Memphis park.

If the circumstances of all these deals are somewhat murky, one is still left with the strong suspicion that Col. Parker had no intention of having his boy compete with anyone. Each Presley film would be a vehicle for its star, period. Parker made no distinction between the films and the other Elvis junk he allowed packagers to merchandise: the necklaces, phonographs, mittens, bracelets, shoes, stuffed hound dogs, pen-pal magazines, toreador pants, Bermuda shorts, ball-point pens, dolls, buttons, colognes, soda pop, bubble-gum cards, board games, pajamas, belts and glow-in-the-dark autographed pictures that were marketed with Elvis' name and likeness without regard to taste or quality.

Superficially, only the music seems immune from Parker's scrap-heap trivialization. Despite the mythology, it isn't true that Elvis became a passionless, affected balladeer after his initial 1954–1956 outburst. Arguably, "Jailhouse Rock," recorded in 1957, is the most powerful piece of rock & roll he ever made. Such tracks as "Rip It Up," "My Baby Left Me," "Blue Suede Shoes," "Paralyzed," "When My Blue Moon Turns to Gold Again," "One Night," "(You're So Square) Baby, I Don't Care," "I Want to Be Free," "Blue Christmas," "Don't," "All Shook Up" and even "Wear My Ring Around Your Neck" (all recorded at RCA, but before Presley joined the Army) rank among Elvis' best music from any period.

Many of these songs exhibit more irony than the Sun sides, and none except "Jailhouse Rock" has the demonic intensity of his very first tracks, but that's reasonable: Not nearly so much was at stake.

Yet, of the thirteen songs mentioned above, only six were originally recorded by Elvis. The rest are covers of relatively recent R&B, country or rockabilly hits. Six winners seems an incredibly prolific output, and it is, but Elvis was operating at the peak of his form; there was no reason for *any* mediocre work in the period between "Heartbreak Hotel" and his departure for Germany. Equally important, of the six great originals listed above, four were written by Leiber and Stoller. Only three (all by Leiber and Stoller) were featured in an Elvis film, and

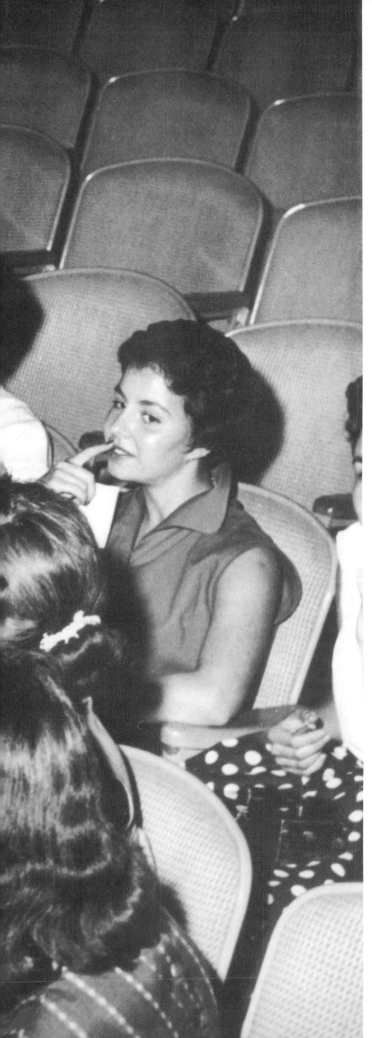

all three appeared in the same picture, *Jailhouse Rock*.

This indicates the weakness of all Elvis' original material, particularly the movie music. Even at this stage, the bulk of the songs Hill and Range provided ranged from mediocre to truly awful. Hill and Range controlled almost all the material that Elvis did on his sessions, but it was much more influential with the soundtrack songs because there were more of them and because cover songs were rarely used in the movies.

Even in Nashville, RCA had ceded its A&R control, normally a label's most jealously guarded prerogative, to the Hill and Range representative, Fred Bienstock. Bienstock, of course, looked out primarily for the best interests of his employers. "We would give out dozens of scripts to writers we had under contract or I thought would do well," Bienstock told Jerry Hopkins. "All the spots where songs went were marked. We asked the writers to submit songs for as many of those spots as they wished."

Such a bald recitation of facts makes the process seem more benign than it really was. Consider, first, the utter hacks who were under contract to Hill and Range, a floating assemblage of names like Roy C. Bennett, Sid Tepper, Bill Giant, Bernie Baum, Florence Kaye, Delores Fuller, Don Robertson, Sid Wayne and Randy Starr, who, in various configurations, wrote dozens of songs for Elvis over a period of more than a decade without ever contributing a memorable note, lyric or lick.

The writers Bienstock felt "would do well" invariably proved to be the ones who would agree to share their publishing proceeds with the Presley music companies that Hill and Range controlled. This applied to Leiber and Stoller, who were already building substantial reputations as R&B writers (they wrote all of the Coasters hits, as well as "Hound Dog" and other Presley hits), Doc Pomus and Mort Shuman, and Aaron Schroeder. At its most extreme, this rapacious policy was even applied to authors of the previously recorded material: Bumps Blackwell, who cowrote Little Richard's hits, has acknowledged that he gave up a portion of his publishing rights in order to reap the greater income a Presley recording guaranteed. (When Elvis discovered what was going on, he

113

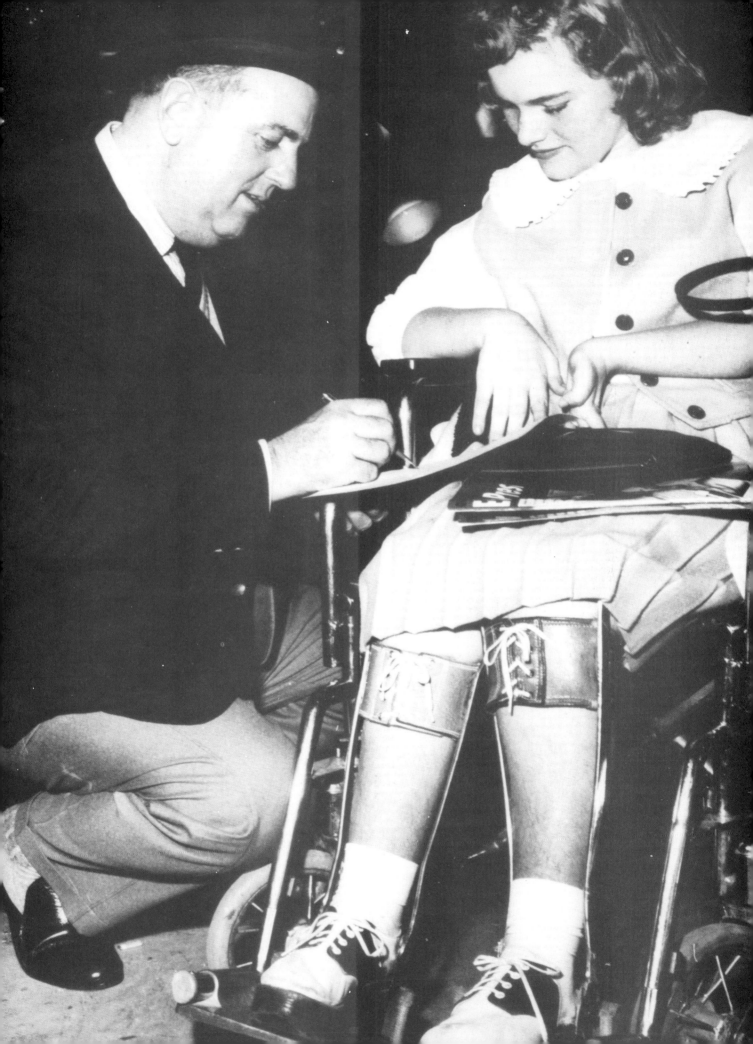

ordered the coercion of writers such as Black-well stopped.)

In the movies, as I have said, this process was exacerbated by the volume of original material required. Additionally, no reputable Hollywood composer could write for a Presley film on speculation, because the composers' guild banned such arrangements. Thus, the hegemony of Hill and Range was solidified, and Elvis was shoved further outside the pale of respectability.

If the soundtrack recordings were lame, the scores of the films themselves were execrable. In *Jailhouse Rock*, the title song is rendered gibberish by an overlay of brass and strings that reduces the number to the bland nothingness of pre-Presley pop. When music figured in the plots of the films, there was even less credibility. In *Loving You*, Elvis' second movie, Wendell Corey plays the leader of a country band. His instrument is a saxophone despite the fact that horns are totally inappropriate to the type of C&W he's supposed to be playing. This displayed a lack of knowledge and sensitivity toward Elvis' musical roots fully the equal of Steve Allen's. If Hollywood had been flying blind, this might have been understandable.

But *Loving You* had a technical adviser—Col. Thomas A. Parker.

Sociologically, Elvis was a constant befuddlement to Hollywood, which meant that the casting and plots of his movies were even more disgraceful than the music. With the exception of *Jailhouse Rock*, all the pre-Army Elvis movies are set in the South. Yet, aside from Elvis, there's not a single character in any of them who speaks like a Southerner. This is especially catastrophic in *King Creole*, which is set in New Orleans. In that film, we are asked to believe not only that Presley's father could be the parsonlike Dean Jagger, the incarnation of the pursed lip, milquetoast Yankee, but that Elvis could be the son of a pharmacist.

Each of the pre-Army movies tries to tap the poor-boy-makes-good mythology that already engulfed Elvis' identity. But the scriptwriters and directors were unable to grasp his central contradictions. Elvis Presley was not a down-and-out refugee of the middle class, like Danny in *King Creole*, and he wasn't a thug, like *Jailhouse Rock*'s Vince Everett, either. This makes the films all the more anomalous. Each of them attempts to establish that Elvis' character, a rebel at the outset, can be assimilated into what passes for the good life, his dreams bought off by mere material success and the ability to *keep to his place*.

This is the purpose of these films. Not simply to diffuse and defuse the original revolutionary, anarchic spirit of Elvis Presley but to use him as the very vehicle which keeps his audience rooted to its place in the status quo, to the concept that the only changes of importance are purely romantic ones (and therefore beyond everyday possibility, except through the magic that had made Elvis Elvis). These films are a denial of the very effort, individual and collective, by which Elvis himself had escaped that status quo. Elvis' dream cannot be denied, so it's simply trivialized out of existence, made into a bauble, the Pink Cadillac used not as symbol but as substance.

The evidence is in the plots themselves. Elvis is always passive, and he is generally dominated by a woman, usually older, but always wealthier and classier. Only rarely is he allowed to

Back home in Memphis, after one of many tours. Preceding pages: Col. Thomas A. Parker does here what he does best.

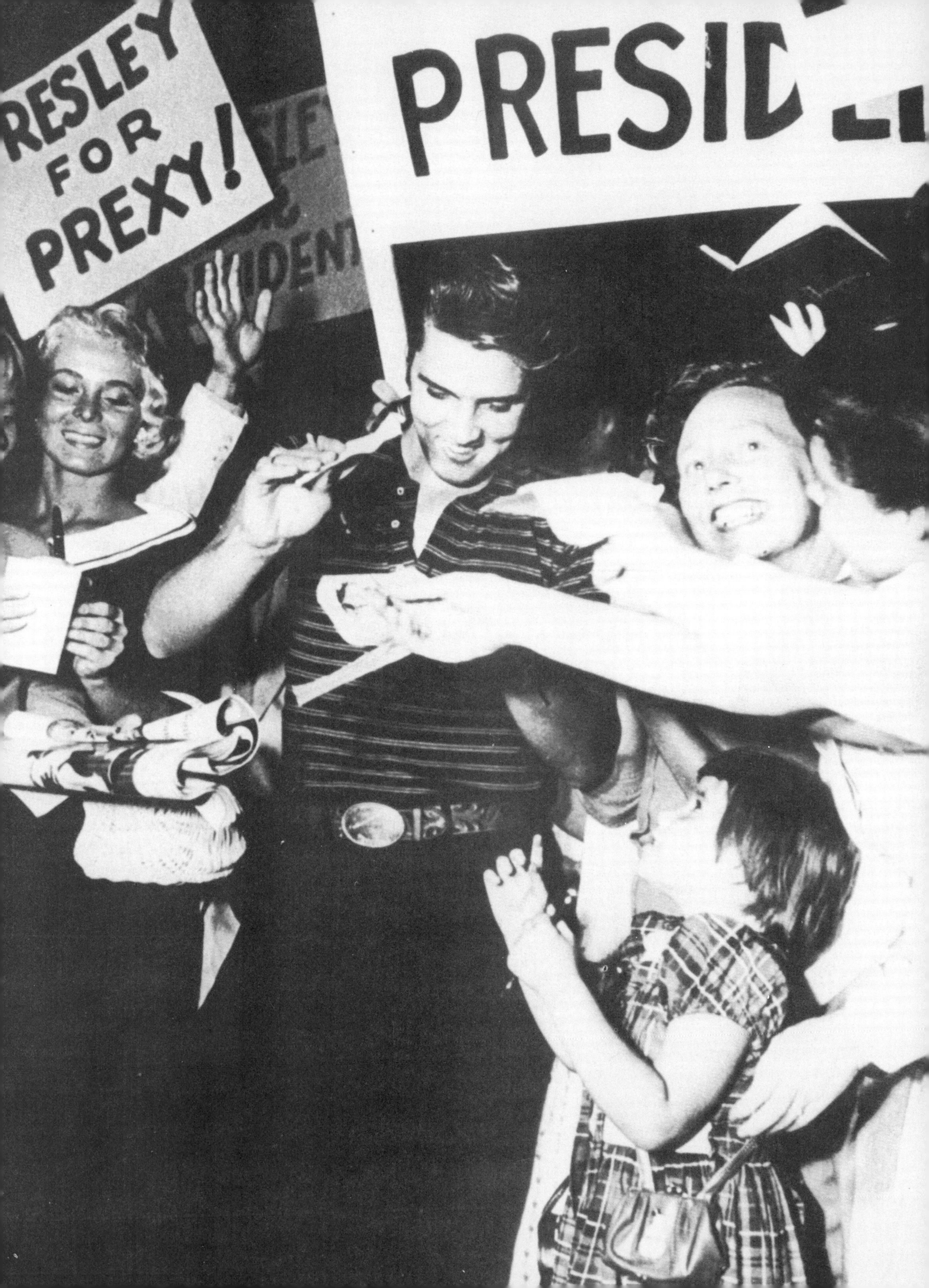
RESLEY
FOR
PREXY!
PRESID

break loose for even a moment. There's that great scene in *Jailhouse Rock* when he grabs Judy Tyler, kisses her until she swoons and then, in response to her complaints, replies, "That ain't tactics, honey, it's just the beast in me." And, even more telling, the throwaway line he delivers to Jagger, his father, in *King Creole*: "You go to school. I'm going out to make a buck."

These are precious moments of truth because they are so rare. The rest of the time, Elvis was prevented from showing himself. In *Jailhouse Rock*, Vince Everett confronts a crowd of suburban intellectuals and he blows up at them, vents his hostility. This is just what the real Elvis never would have done. He knew his depth, and he knew that in Hollywood he was out of it. But what could he do?

Lloyd Shearer, a writer/photographer doing a story for *Life*, suggested to Elvis that he delay signing his film contract and go to college instead. Recounting the story in a magazine article twenty years later, Shearer remembered, "He looked at me with amazement. 'I don't 'spect,' he said, 'you ever been poor. We Presleys—we been poor as far back as I can remember.'" Shearer did not understand that he was being patronizing, apparently, much less that Elvis had just let him in on the entire secret of his seeming passivity about his own career. The psychology is, in fact, very simple: He viewed the movies, like the music, as a job. If it gave him what he wanted, he was happy to meet all of its requirements. If it also robbed him of his self-respect, he would be disturbed, but he would never refuse to work, much less quit. "When he blew up, he blew up inside," said Gordon Stoker. In other words, that ain't tactics, honey, it's just the naïve urchin in him.

This mentality meant nothing to Hollywood, where most people relate to poverty as something that happens to others, or used to happen, or perhaps is a state of being temporarily without funds. Generations of economic hopelessness are not ordinarily found in the backgrounds of directors, actors or screenwriters. So Elvis became literally unbelievable to them, and since he was himself essentially mute on all cre-

A winter aerial view of Graceland, the 23-room Memphis mansion Elvis bought in March 1957. Elvis later painted it so that it shone in the dark.

121

ative topics and since his manager made a fetish out of caring only for the bottom line, he was even more defenseless in Hollywood than in music or TV.

After his return from the Army in 1960, Elvis became a cartoon character. But he was not protected or given the careful dignity and respect Walt Disney reserved for a cartoon superstar like Mickey Mouse or even for an animated second banana like Donald Duck. Elvis was handled like Goofy, an expendable dummy who could be cloned and turned into whatever sort of dim-witted goon his masters demanded.

In 1962 he made *Follow That Dream*, a title that should have encapsulated his incarnation of the American Dream. Instead, the plot called for Elvis to portray Toby Kwimper, based on the hillbilly caricature Li'l Abner, a creature of brute strength and a little common sense but totally without maturity or even a glimmer of intellect. Elvis sang the title song with his back to the camera.

Since 1956, fans had swarmed the Presley home and often stolen bits of brick and grass. In 1957 the Music Gates were built at Graceland.

"Well, it seems like I have played the game your way too long. And it seems the game I've played has made you strong."
—*Jimmy Cliff, "Trapped"*

Superficially, Elvis' goals had been realized. He was a star of stage, screen, radio, television and recordings, easily the biggest name in American entertainment, an international figure so persuasively attractive that in other lands, young people had begun to dream of the U.S. as the land where anyone might grow up to become not president but Presley, ruler of his own destiny. But Elvis' acts of self-invention were unwelcome at home. In addition to the media and social forces allied against the outbreak of hillbilly barbarism, there stood the United States government's Selective Service System. Military conscription was an effective weapon against uppity new celebrities, as had already been proven with the unconventional World Series heroes, Billy Martin and Johnny Podres, who were immediately drafted after their moments of glory. Even though Elvis had become famous, there was nothing to prevent the draft from being used as a weapon to put him back in his place. As the head of the Memphis draft board saw it: "After all, when you take him out of the entertainment business, what have you got left? A truckdriver." In the America of which Elvis dreamed, that would have been enough distinction for anyone, but in the land where he lived, such status was not only a liability but an indictment.

It's not surprising that Elvis created no stir as his induction neared; he asked only for a sixty-day deferment to complete *King Creole*. He never objected to being pulled out of his career at such an inopportune time. Elvis was a rebel by instinct more than by choice, and, at least in his eyes, his rebellion of style never conflicted with being the most naïve sort of "good citizen." Elvis wasn't eager to join the service but he also refused to buy his way out. He was offered special deals by the Marines and Navy

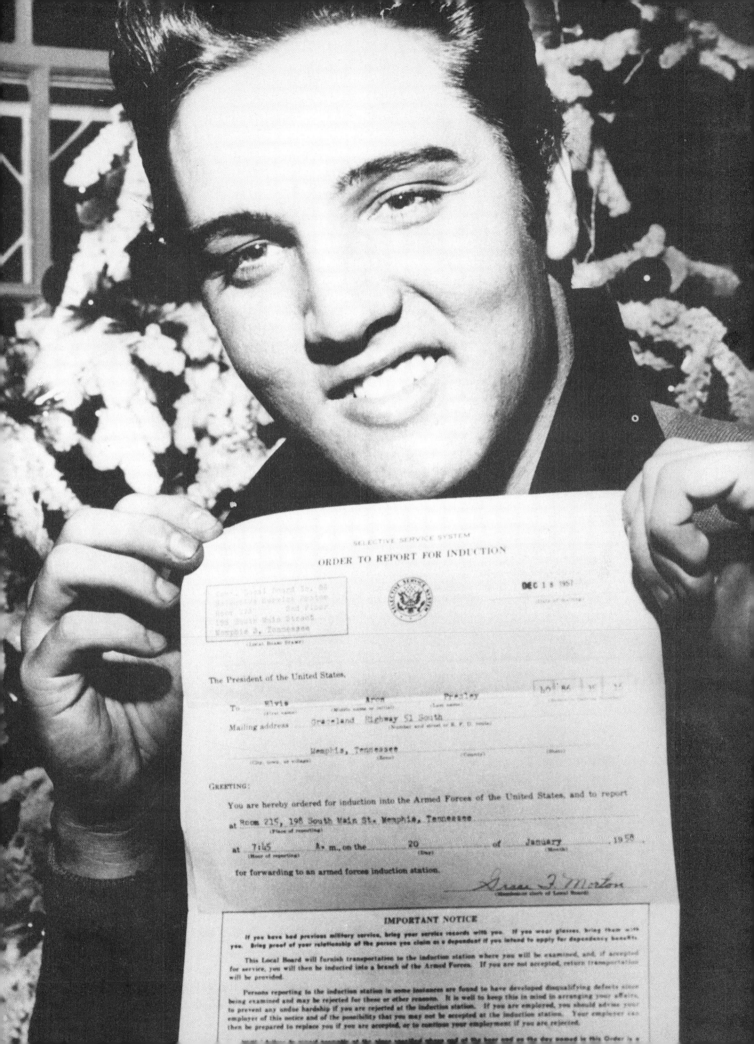

if he would enlist before being called up in the draft, and once he was in the Army, he refused to join the special forces as an entertainer. This should not come as too much of a surprise. If he was unwilling to complain about terrible songs and crappy film scripts, Elvis wasn't about to go against the government itself.

Yet the government's intention in drafting Elvis was to rob him of everything—not just fame but also his wealth and whatever new dignity he had acquired (as is made clear in contemporary accounts of the Memphis draft board proceedings). Certainly, the least the draft board expected was that making Presley an infantry grunt would eliminate his unholy arrogance. More significantly, experience suggested that a pop celebrity's fame was, at best, transient and that Elvis' was probably more transient than most because it was based on the sexual fantasies of adolescent girls who would most likely outgrow their obsession by the time he was released from the Army in early 1960.

Ironically, it was just these women who ensured that Elvis would reenter civilian life as much a star as he left it. From the moment he was sent off, locks shorn, blue suede shoes locked up, first to Texas and then to West Germany, these fans maintained an obsession so keen that it was all Parker, RCA and the film producers and merchandisers could do to meet

their demand for trinkets, recordings and icons.

The continuing devotion of his fans—especially his female fans—is one of the most miraculous aspects of the Elvis legend. Unlike Frank Sinatra, Elvis didn't rise from the ashes of adolescent infatuation sporting a new, "mature" style, because he never lost the rapt attention of the core of his audience. Elvis did not move all at once or stealthily from one mode of musical and sexual expression to another. He transformed himself over time, continuing the broadening process that had begun as soon as he escaped Sam Phillips' restrictions. And his fans stayed with him.

Yet the loyalty of his audience imposed its own restrictions on Elvis. He may have sung like a rhythm & blues singer (Ray Charles is the only singer of his era who is comparable in range of talent and ambition), but he was marketed using the techniques and devices of country & western. After he entered the Army, his audience began more and more to resemble the country fans described by Chet Flippo in *Your Cheatin' Heart*, a biography of Hank Williams: "... the country-music fan was unlike any other music fan or, for that matter, any celebrity fan that the United States had produced. The country-music fan asked few things of his hero, or her hero—for women were the backbone of the country audience—but those few things had to be delivered." The breaking point of this loyalty, explains Flippo, came only when the performer "quit being just a singing representative of [his] peers and started putting on airs."

This relationship was inevitably hypocritical. The country fan did not ask that his star continue to appear impoverished or reject the trappings of success. Nor was the country star obliged to make statements of regret at his estrangement from the workaday world. (Those are the demands of bohemian audiences.) What the country fan wanted was something impossible: that the pampered, expensively clad, luxuriously transported, well-endowed and shrewdly invested star should maintain exactly the same mentality that he and the fan originally shared, that his view of the world should not be altered by the loft of his perch. The effect was pernicious and pathetic not only because it

The first Christmas at Graceland brought gifts from fans and a draft notice from the Army. This page and overleaf: exams and induction.

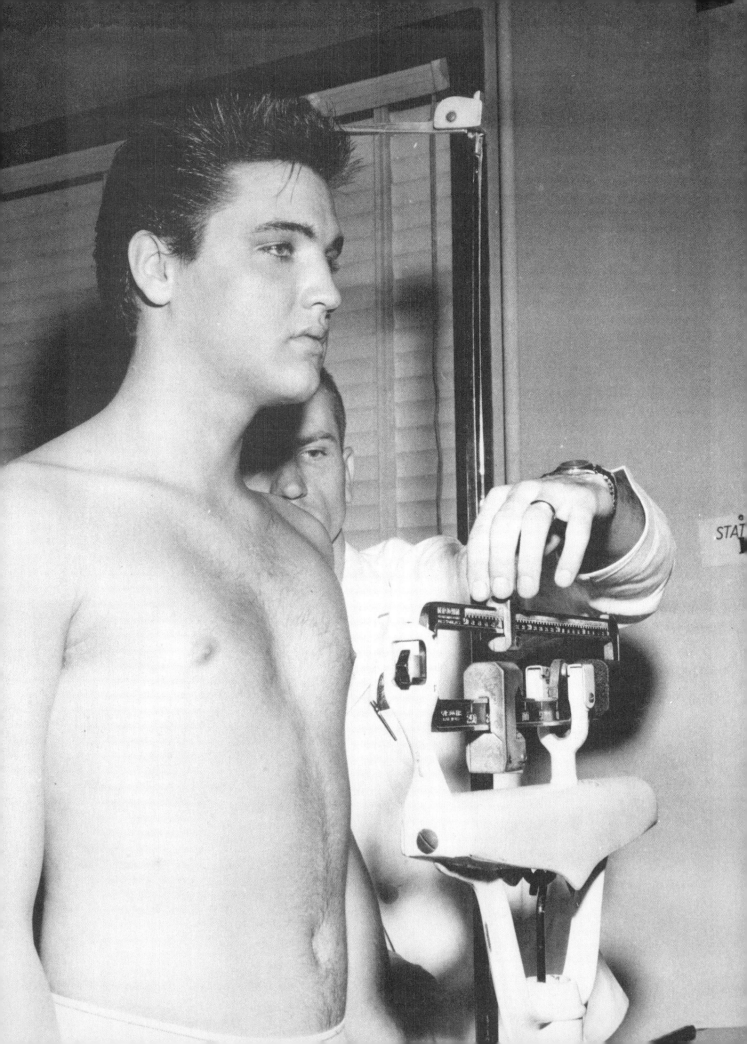

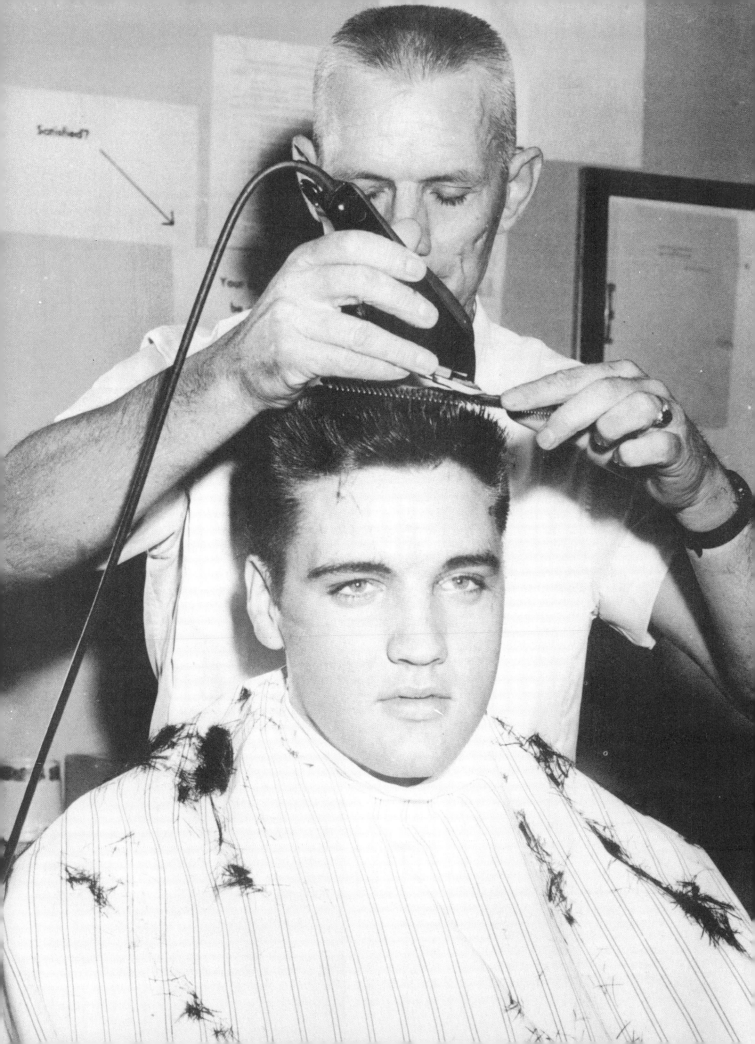

prevented the star from ever making explicit criticisms of the conditions that kept his audience impoverished but because it kept the audience from ever seeing the truth about the human consequences of a change in economic status. The result was a culture that was steeped in vicariousness and utterly passive—and as more Southerners moved into urban America, seeking work during and after World War II, these attitudes came to epitomize working-class attitudes to *all* culture.

Elvis was a product of this culture of passivity, but he was also a well-informed voice in opposition to it—one of the few who spoke with the real credibility of an insider, neither a patronizing, moralistic leftist reformer nor an equally patronizing, moralistic right-wing demagogue. What Elvis did was suggest, especially to younger listeners, that there were more attractive options than the limited ones they already knew about, and that these options were reachable *without essential compromise*. Although few ever took Elvis up on even a portion of his implicit challenge, many permanently honored and revered him for his personal breakout.

By the time he returned home from the Army, Elvis' audience had doubled back on him. In addition to celebrating his victory, fans also demanded, as the price of their loyalty, that he behave according to prevailing standards, that he cease challenging them and begin delivering safe and platitudinous doses of the already known. Elvis' fans caged him much more effectively than the record companies, movie moguls, TV censors, song publishers or even the military could have hoped to do. Because Elvis had never escaped the employee mentality, he related to the audience as his boss. His own needs and desires were, if not entirely subordinate, beside the point.

Had Elvis been the same defiant but resilient lad who'd encountered Marion Keisker at Sun Records, he might have found a way to retain his artistic mobility along with his money and his fame. But Elvis was not the same person. He hadn't made too many compromises, but he had sat idly while too many compromises were

made. And he had become accustomed to a relatively easy life while never losing sight of what the other side was like. He was not about to chance losing it all now. So he accepted the limits imposed by his audience, denying that he had changed with his success—and, because he was Elvis and therefore one of the most honest if befuddled creatures on the face of the planet, he really tried not to change. Ultimately this meant that he hid not only from the superficial enticements of Beverly Hills but also from any new ideas and experiences, even from people who were in frequent contact with such things. His insurrection was over; an armistice had been made.

If Elvis needed additional incentive to cease his rebellion, the Army offered it, though not through military discipline. As Elvis knew it, the Army was a cracker institution, run by rednecks and good ol' boys, poor whites and near-trash, like his original self; that was the mid-Fifties reality of the private soldiers' Army. Placing Elvis in such an institution for two years was the surest way to convince him that he must never turn back from mammon, that while dignity might be expendable, comfort was not.

There wasn't anywhere to turn, even if he

had sought an alternative. Elvis had gone as far as American individualism could take him, and he had not found any community willing to accept him on his terms, or any community to whose terms he could conform. At this stage, Elvis had become very much like John Wayne at the end of *The Searchers*, John Ford's magnificent 1956 Western—a man who has rescued his society from the most predatory evils but cannot bring himself to live within that society.

Elvis was stranded. His mother had died, which was a trauma, and his father had remarried, which was another, and he had fallen in love with a fourteen-year-old girl, a relationship even more gothic than the one he'd had with his mother. The Army was exactly the kind of hierarchical community that had pinned him down before he'd become famous, and yet the only outside group that indicated that Elvis might be acceptable on *any* terms was the world of Future Homemakers of America, which comprised the bulk of his loyal fans. Colonel Parker was living out his own mythology of greed: fast bucks and damn the consequences. The community of cronies Elvis had begun to assemble —the nascent Memphis Mafia—was full of buffoons, yes-men, gold-diggers and dull thugs. Elvis dreamed as big as anyone in history had dared and he was surrounded by the most small-time sidekicks that any great man has known. So he was finally, truly alone. And not simply alone, but encircled.

Picture Elvis imprisoned, locked inside dark, somber, massive walls. On a beautifully moonlit night, he brazenly slips over the wall, snapping free easily. And as he stops—for just an *instant* —to drink in his new freedom, to savor how simple it had been, to gape in awe at the prospect stretched out before him, he hesitates a moment too long, and as he turns for one last glance at the walls that no longer encircle him, new fences are already going up around him. Elvis had more space now, but he had lost the totality of freedom he had known for one moment. Now, he seemed to be free only from a distance; up close, he was obviously trapped. He was, of course, allowed to act as if he chose to keep things this way. But Elvis himself knew better; the boundaries were perfectly clear to his eyes. It would be a long time before he even thought about breaching them again . . . and

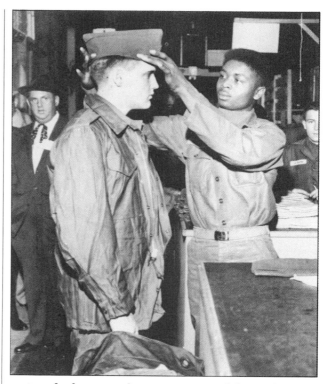

not only because he was trapped but also because, in retrospect, it seemed that freedom had made him dizzy. He was no longer certain that so much freedom was what he needed.

At each instant of victory, Elvis had been spurned, so that not the triumph but its joy had leaked away. He was not rockabilly enough for Sam Phillips nor country enough for Jim Denny; he was too unsophisticated for Steve Allen and too sexy for Ed Sullivan; he was not suave enough for Hollywood and too damn reckless for his own most avid fans. In his multiplicity, he was incomprehensible to all of them at least some of the time, and they shrank in fear of his complexity and then returned to attack him, to reduce him to dimensions within their grasp.

Who can believe Elvis ever forgot that when he reenacted the American Dream the response of America was not an effusive welcome but a lust to rub his nose in the inescapable fact that he was nothing but a hick? "After all, when you take him out of the entertainment business, what have you got left? A truckdriver."

Elvis could play humble. It was his best role. But only because he knew that he had every reason to *be* humble, that (barring his remarkable talent) there was nothing to prevent any man of sufficient guts and vision from doing what he had done. Before this fact, even his unfathomable arrogance crumbled.

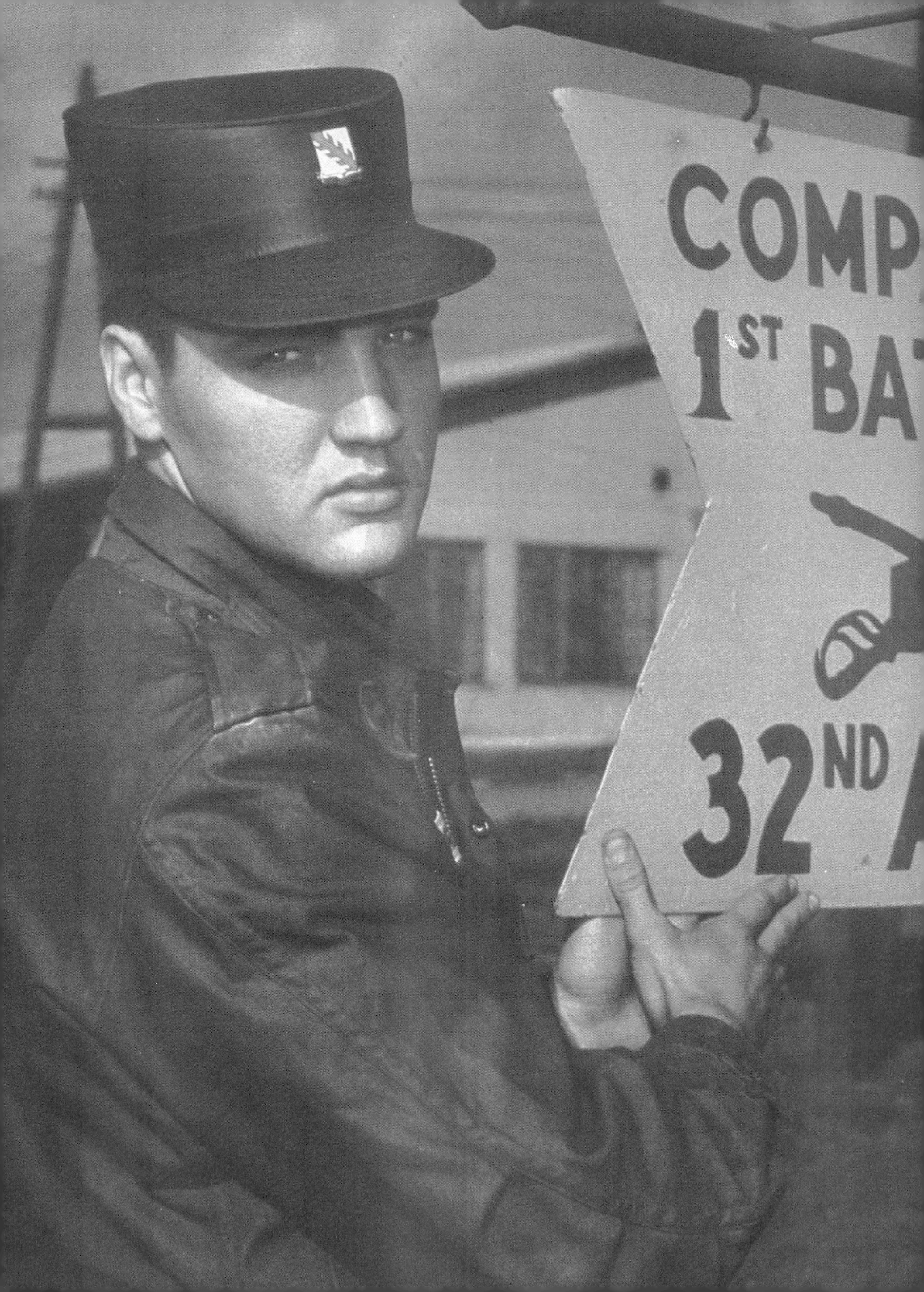
COMP
1ST BAT
32ND A

"*Thought it was a nightmare,
   Lord, it was so true.
*T*hey told me don't go walkin'
   slow,
Devil's on the loose
Better run through the jungle,
Better run through the jungle,
Better run through the jungle,
Oh don't look back at me."*
                    —*John Fogerty,*
             "*Run through the Jungle*"

n the myth, Elvis' career dove straight downward from the day he entered the Army. There was, of course, the brief, inexplicable flare-up of genius in 1968–1969 when he managed, in the space of only a few months, a magnificent television special, a volcanic return to Las Vegas, a trio of classic recordings, and an all-conquering national concert tour. Otherwise, however, these were the years in which Elvis, numbed and gorged, surrounded himself with toadies and stooges. Most of all, this was the period in which Elvis ground out demeaning movies and music with a monotony that was both awful and awesome. As fiction, this might have been an acceptable scenario. It's a little romantic, not terribly well conceived. Still the magic of that glorious TV special might have put it over.

But Elvis was a real man and his work was the product of an artist who somehow, by God's grace or sheer tenacity, pushed himself through the greatest heaps of schlock one man ever endured. His comeback was no overnight reversal nor was it an isolated instance of magic. If a skilled observer had been paying close attention all along, the 1968 comeback might have seemed anything but unlikely—though it couldn't have been a whit less stunning.

It's little wonder that no such observer existed. The films that were the bulk of Elvis' work from 1960 until 1968 would tax the atten-

Left: Elvis was stationed in Bad Nauheim, West Germany.

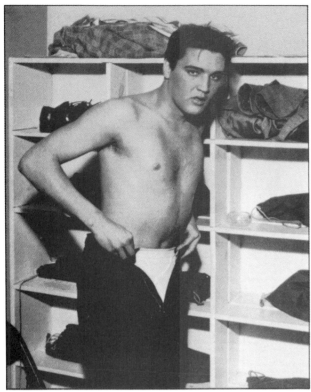

tion span of God's own messenger. There are twenty-eight of them, and for every *Flaming Star*, intelligently directed by Don Siegel, there are six or seven travesties as completely inept as *Fun in Acapulco* and *Girls! Girls! Girls!* These movies, the weakest series of star vehicles in Hollywood history, "all have two things in common," wrote Stanley Booth. "None lost money, none is contingent at any point upon reality."

There was little hope for these films from the beginning. Elvis, the central figure, was regarded—by cast and crew—as a clod and a clown, a hick and a hillbilly, a money machine. Anyway, no one, no matter how talented, could have kept up this astonishing, crippling pace: three films a year for seven years without regard for quality of script or score, direction or supporting cast. Given the inhospitable environment, these films might have been planned to rob Elvis of his vitality.

"Well, there's nobody that helps you out," Elvis told one interviewer. "They have a director for the scenes, as far as the acting, and as far as the singing and all, you're on your own. Nobody tells you how to do that, you have to learn it yourself."

This statement is a bit less opaque than most of Elvis' other gestures at explaining himself.

He tells us that he knows he is abandoned (but refuses to admit the degree), that he is aware that his films are only an excuse for the songs, and then he lets us in on a little secret: This music is different. You have to *learn* to sing it.

The Elvis movies have the least music in them of any musical comedies ever made. Not that there aren't a great many songs—there's just precious little music to them. The titles are pathetic: "(There's) No Room to Rhumba in a Sports Car," "Song of the Shrimp," "Fort Lauderdale Chamber of Commerce." Who could sing such drool and make it stick? Who could put across such drivel and keep the customers lined up for more?

Only Elvis. But Elvis was not content with carny tricks. He took the miracle to its extreme; he seized each song that possessed a glimmer of worth and wrung out its full potential. The catch is that Elvis sings the hell out of even these ridiculously titled songs. They remain lousy songs—but his performances are anything but. On the rare occasions when he was given superior material, Elvis was still a revelatory performer, quite capable of astonishing performances. Listen to "Crying in the Chapel," "King of the Whole Wide World," "Viva Las Vegas." Though the soundtrack albums come so close to worthlessness that they are absolutely chilling, and the other LPs are not much better, Elvis redeems each of them in the end.

Elvis' LP catalogue is a jumble in which he seems barely involved. True, in 1960, faced with the challenge of reconquering his audience upon his return from the Army, he summoned up a burst of creative zeal and delivered a fine LP, *Elvis Is Back*. After that, he seems to have been willing to sing almost anything that was placed in front of him, as if campaigning for membership in the musical clean-plate club. But he displayed not even passing interest in the endgame chores of album making (final song selection, sequencing, mixing, mastering). Maybe he was never made aware of the importance of such details—but by now he was also plain lazy, fat and sassy, *satisfied*.

The result is not only records that are technically erratic and sometimes downright amateurish but a recorded catalogue that is an un-

Right: one of the last pictures taken of the family together. Overleaf: keeping track, and relaxing with Margit Buergin, an occasional date.

136

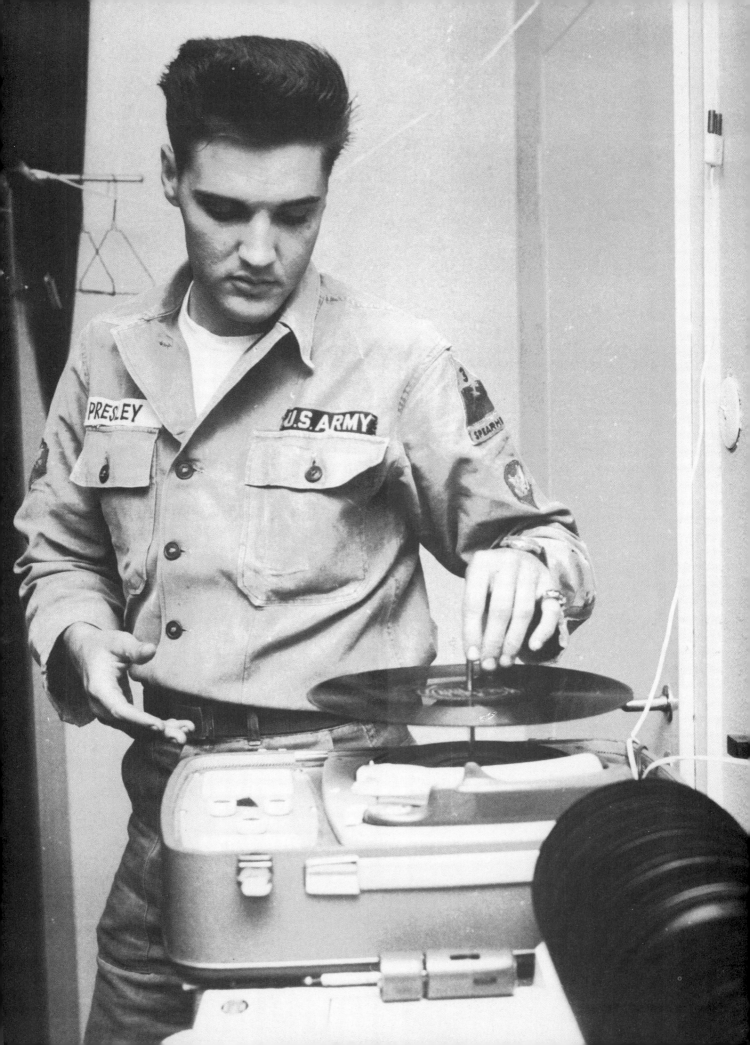

trustworthy representation of his work, a meaningless hodgepodge of vinyl. So, to understand the music of this period, you take Elvis track by track, if you take him at all. And then you're faced with the chore of sifting the gold from the dross, something RCA, Hill and Range and Col. Parker never bothered to do, for the most obvious reason: None of them stood to gain anything from superior Presley performances since mediocre ones sold equally well. Indeed, the business interests and Elvis himself had a great deal to lose when he was at his best, since each great record raised expectations for the next, and made clear the absolute callowness of the great junky mass that underpinned the career.

Perhaps that's why the most treacherous albums of all are volumes three and four of RCA's *Golden Records* series. Certainly, these albums make more sense as deliberately slipshod attempts to sabotage Elvis' reputation than as accurate documents of his best and biggest hits. They omit four of the best and best-selling records he made in this period: "Viva Las Vegas," "Can't Help Falling in Love with You," "Return to Sender" and "One Broken Heart for Sale." The *Golden Records* collections also ignore all of the gospel recordings, even the Number One hit "Crying in the Chapel." (No wonder that in *Mystery Train*, Greil Marcus uses the *Golden Records* as evidence that Elvis' output in the early and middle Sixties bordered on worthlessness.)

Beyond these obvious omissions, there are unheralded treasures hidden in the Elvis EPs and LPs of the early Sixties: "King of the Whole Wide World," "C'mon Everybody," "Reconsider Baby," "Make Me Know It," "Follow That Dream" and "Such a Night" are the cream. Stack these with the best tracks from the *Golden Records* themselves ("Little Sister," "(Marie's the Name) His Latest Flame," "Stuck on You," "Fame and Fortune," "I Feel So Bad," "Are You Lonesome Tonight," "She's Not You," "(You're the) Devil in Disguise," "Ain't That Loving You Baby " and "A Mess of Blues") and the result is a brand new perspective on Elvis' work from this period. Rather than endless tepid mediocrity we can spot more than two dozen songs of quality, and at least

half a dozen masterpieces. This outpouring is almost unmatched in the pop music of the period immediately preceding the Beatles. Only Roy Orbison, Ray Charles, Jackie Wilson and a few Motown artists can challenge Elvis for both quality and quantity of music in this period, and only Charles can touch his diversity.

Given the disadvantages he worked with, Elvis' creativity during this time is even more remarkable. He did not have a supportive environment, as the Motown artists did; indeed, he had to struggle both against his own complacency and that of advisers and cronies grown fat on the status quo. Also, Elvis achieved these musical results while churning out two or three movies, at least two albums, an EP and various singles each year. Given these obstacles, it is fair to say that the music mentioned above comprises one of the most marvelous and inexplicable creations of Elvis' career. These records don't merely replay and elaborate upon the music Elvis made in the Fifties, they extend it.

In fact, the mark of Presley's creativity from 1960 through 1965 is the diverse explorations

Elvis met Priscilla Beaulieu in West Germany in 1959; she was then 14, the adopted daughter of an Army major.

Moving up: Elvis gets
his sergeant's stripes.

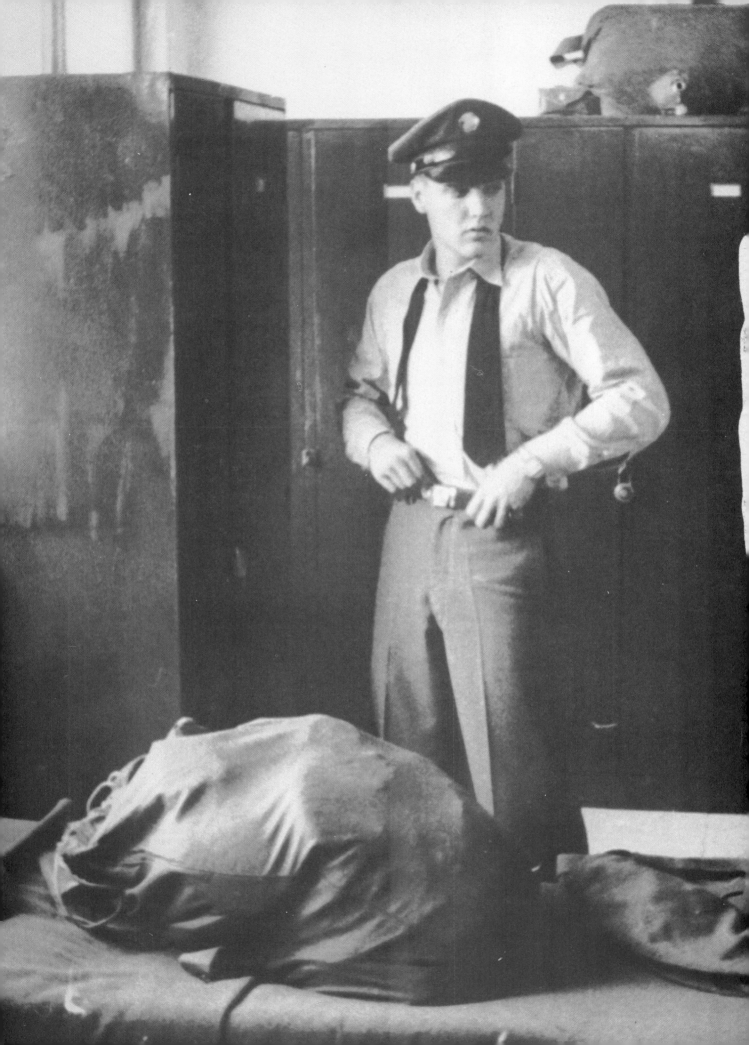

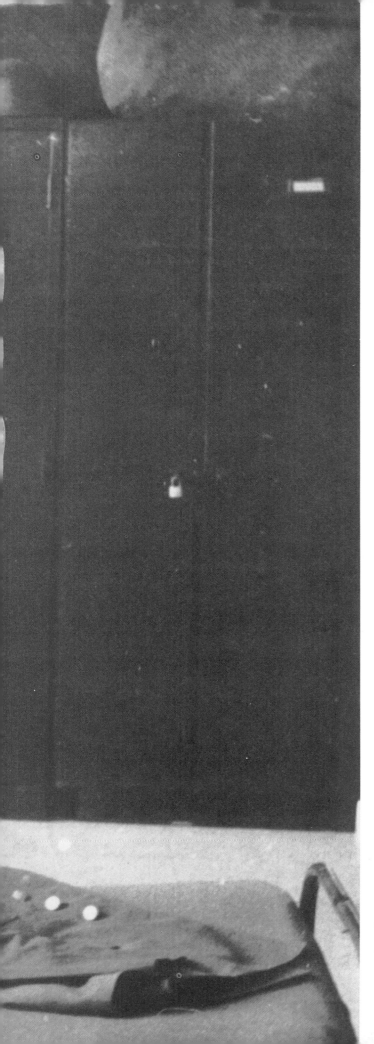

such recordings make. "Little Sister" is rock hard, a stinging stomp, while on "Viva Las Vegas," Presley makes rock & roll swing in the best sense. "Fame and Fortune" is delivered with such absolutely ironic cool that it seems almost a parody of conventional ballad singing —but Elvis earned his right to that parody with the breathtaking purity of "Can't Help Falling in Love with You." Few of the songs Elvis recorded in the early and middle Sixties are blues, but blues informs almost everything here. The version of "What'd I Say" that appears in *Viva Las Vegas* establishes Elvis' continuing mastery of the basic idiom, while "She's Not You" integrates the Jordanaires so completely, it's practically doo-wop.

These songs come from perverse and diverse sources: The otherwise useless Giant-Baum-Kaye team, possibly Hill and Range's worst, actually summoned up "(You're the) Devil in Disguise" while the best of the Hill and Range writers, Doc Pomus and Mort Shuman, created a series of what became the very best of the era's Presley music: "Viva Las Vegas," "Little Sister," "(Marie's the Name) His Latest Flame," "A Mess of Blues" and some others. Doc Pomus probably put it best when he said that of all the people who sang his songs, only Elvis taught him something new about each of them.

These performances may not have the weight of the ones Elvis did at Sun, but they make up for it with smooth assurance. Not all of them are rock & roll, but the rock that's here is fantastic, driving and compelling. Perhaps Elvis doesn't sing as if much is at stake, but then, nothing much *is* at stake. Anyway, he still glides unfailingly to the guts of "King of the Whole Wide World." And when he sings "Crying in the Chapel," he is everything he ever thought he could be. This music lacks the drama of the Fifties music. But that's because what we're hearing is not genius discovering itself but the sound of genius at work.

So Elvis' Sixties music does represent a sort of decline; it's just that it takes him a good deal longer to bottom out than the legend contends. *Elvis Is Back* so easily reaffirmed his dominance of American popular music in 1960 that he sim-

Overleaf: Vernon and Elvis going to see Gladys at Methodist Hospital in Memphis, and later on the steps of Graceland after her death. At the funeral Elvis cried, "Oh, God, everything I have is gone."

ply cruised, trying less and less with each successive season, as though testing to see how little he could deliver and remain King.

To make matters worse, the RCA/Hill and Range formula continued to narrow his audience, which took its toll commercially as well as artistically. After 1960, Elvis did not place a song on the country charts for eight years, and after "(You're the) Devil in Disguise," in 1963, he never again found a place on the rhythm & blues charts. His audience was being reduced to a set of fans content merely to hear his voice singing any tripe, no matter how unmitigated.

In late 1963, when the Beatles began their assault on America, they presented the first serious challenge to Presley's reign. Whether the Beatles became bigger than Elvis isn't especially relevant—the Beatles probably sold more records, but Elvis matched the entire quartet's charisma on his own. The Beatles damaged El-

vis far more, however, by reestablishing rock & roll as a visionary and idealistic medium. It was as if only the Beatles, and the best of the other bands that trailed behind them in the British Invasion, recalled the distinctly American promise Elvis had first represented. And it was this reminder of possibility that the Beatles and the British Invasion reawakened in the American rock audience.

For half a decade, Elvis had coasted on craft and confidence. During that time he had been able to count on every one of his albums—and almost all of his singles—making the Top Ten. But in 1965, the year the British Invasion took hold as a revolution in taste, not just a fad, he had only one Top Ten single, "Crying in the Chapel," which he had recorded nearly five years earlier. His albums fell to the bottom of the Top Ten.

Yet 1965 was not so bad compared to the next three years, which were the closest Elvis ever came to knowing public indifference. In 1966, RCA issued four singles, but only "Love Letters," a remake of a Ketty Lester R&B hit, made the Top Twenty (squeaking in at Nineteen); Elvis' three albums of that year, all soundtracks, ranked only in the lower ranges of the Top Twenty. Compared to 1967, though, 1966 was a year of good fortune. RCA kept to its saturation-release schedule, with four singles and three albums. But the bottom had dropped out of the Elvis market: The highest-charting single was "Indescribably Blue," at Thirty-three; of the others, only "Big Boss Man" cracked the Top Forty. Elvis' highest-charting album was the gospel set, *How Great Thou Art*. The other two albums of that year were soundtracks; *Clambake* managed to make it to Number Forty, but *Double Trouble* crapped out at Forty-seven. And, even though Elvis' third 1968 single, "U.S. Male," snuck in at Number Twenty-eight, the rest of his releases that year were even more disastrous than those of 1966 and 1967: "You'll Never Walk Alone," a preposterous version of the sappy standard issued in April, bottomed out at Ninety, and none of the rest touched Top Forty. Until the unexpected success of his TV soundtrack album, *Elvis!*, at Christmastime, the album charts

Getting out: Elvis returns to Memphis, March 1960 after two years away. "The Army sure changed me, but I can't tell offhand, how."

148

looked equally dire.

In truth, Elvis deserved his commercial fate. His only non-soundtrack-album releases of this period are the lugubrious *Golden Records, Volume Four*, the lackluster *Elvis for Everyone*, with its pedestrian remakes of everything from Chuck Berry's "Memphis, Tennessee" to Hank Williams' "Your Cheatin' Heart," and the glorious but hardly mainstream *How Great Thou Art*. And even *How Great Thou Art*, devoted to stiff and formal hymn singing, suffers in comparison to Elvis' 1960 gospel LP, *His Hand in Mine*. The soundtrack LPs of these years (*Girl Happy, Harum Scarum, Frankie and Johnny, Paradise Hawaiian Style, Double Trouble, Clambake*) are the least inspired recordings Elvis—or maybe anyone—ever made.

This decline wasn't all Elvis' fault. He was burdened with a bloodless, inefficient production system, incapable of delivering material of sufficient quality to succeed in a newly competitive marketplace. Hill and Range had always worked at cross-purposes with Elvis, but they and all of the other old-time publishers were now in major trouble because the important new writers (Lennon and McCartney, Jagger and Richards, Bob Dylan, Paul Simon) rarely needed old-fashioned publishers to find singers

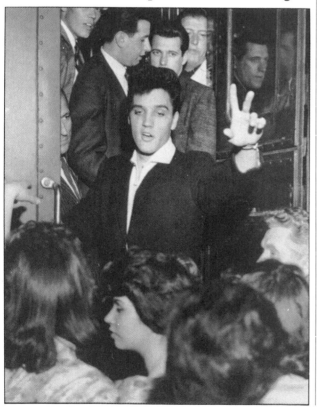

for their songs. The best new writers were performers themselves. The few contract writers of quality (teams like Gerry Goffin and Carole King, Ellie Greenwich and Jeff Barry, Barry Mann and Cynthia Weil) worked with rock-oriented publishers like Don Kirshner. Often these writers were also producers and on occasion they performed as well.

This new shape of things was problematic for every nonwriting singer. Most suffered more than Elvis. At least he had his incredible reputation, an established audience of loyalists and the avowed admiration of the Beatles themselves to fall back on. ("Before there was Elvis, there was nothing," said John Lennon.)

But Elvis could not escape the most important consequences of the British-led pop-music revolution. Younger listeners were after novelty above all, as an antidote to a static and predictable music scene. Far from seeming a revolutionary, Elvis now seemed the firmest pillar of the status quo—especially to the young Beatlemaniacs who hadn't been around for his original conquests. Elvis was stuck in the musical middle—a middle fast disintegrating in the face of the mid-Sixties shock troops of pop.

The Beatles also received the enthusiasm of just those Elvis fans who had been most confused and alienated by his conservatism since he returned from the Army. Many of these fans had been indifferent to pop music in the intervening years, but their casual interest was probably the difference between Elvis making the Top Ten and scraping into the Top Forty. And it was just these fans, the most sophisticated part of the Elvis audience of the Fifties, who were leading the Sixties rock movement—not only performers like Lennon and Dylan but a million other listeners who responded with unprecedented enthusiasm to pop music that was imbued with dreams and ambition once again.

Elvis' isolation, his cocooned existence among the hustlers and Memphis Mafia yes-men, had hardly prepared him for an upsurge of rock music based on the emotions and ideals he himself had first stirred. But, however improbably, here it was again. This time, though, the performers would not sell out so easily. Indeed, they said from time to time that they did not

Elvis is back, more popular than ever: "As for the fans, they changed some," he said, "but they were still there."

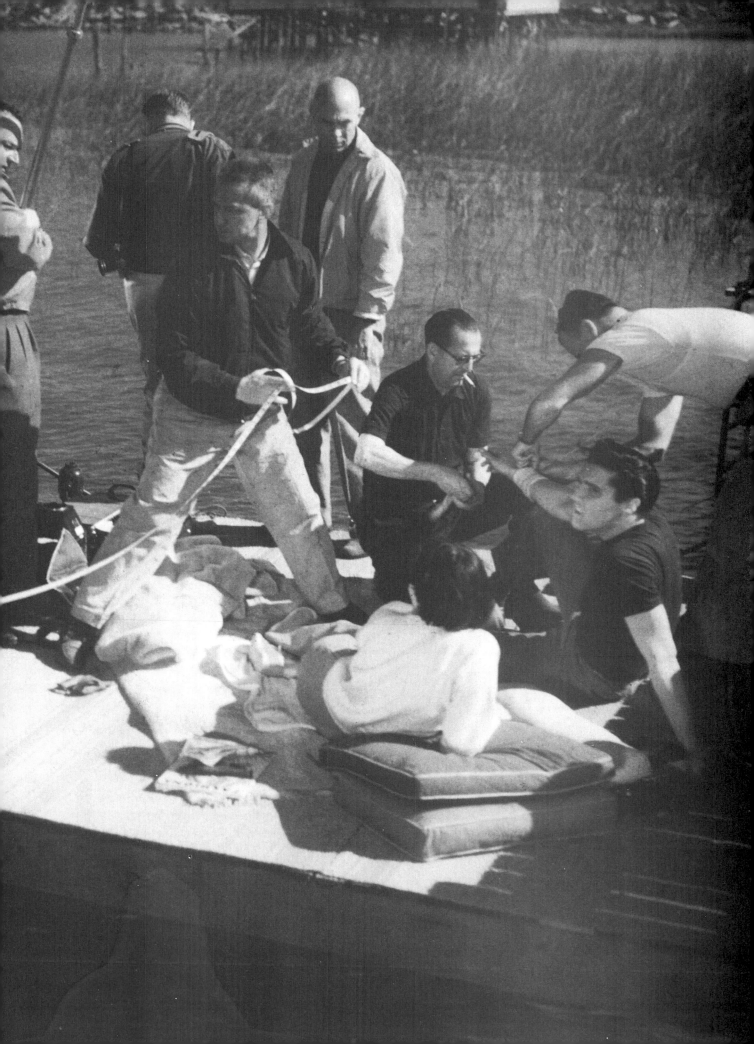

want to "end up like Elvis," trapped in the web of old-fogey show biz. They said this with respect—Elvis had, in his way, given them their start after all—but they said it firmly. Elvis had mapped not only the route to success but also its most significant and deadly pitfalls.

Joining the revived rock & roll movement wasn't a likely option, either. Even if he'd wanted to, Elvis no longer had that much mobility. Hill and Range and RCA had to fight the British bands, which were eroding not only the Presley business but all that was left of pre–rock & roll popular music. Neither the record company nor the publisher was likely to encourage Elvis—their last beachhead against the changing economics of the music business—to convert to the enemy side.

Anyway, Elvis didn't have a single adviser with the imagination to suggest that he make an album of Beatles, Dylan and Stones songs or perhaps record an album using those stars as sidemen. Like the pop-music moguls Elvis had rendered obsolete in the Fifties, the men behind Elvis wanted to proceed as if the Beatles and the British Invasion represented nothing more than a fad that would soon fade away. They pretended that nothing fundamental had changed when, in fact, everything had.

But there's no reason to think Elvis would have been especially eager to record with Beatles-generation musicians, anyhow. Elvis wanted to be a great vocalist; the new music was so completely band-oriented that the only significant solo performer launched in this era, Bob Dylan, was unable to reach any kind of commercial peak without joining forces with the Hawks (later the Band), a group of near-equal ability.

Elvis' greatest ambition was to unify all of the popular music he heard around him yet to keep the synthesis within the comfortable bounds of the society in which he'd been raised. The ambition of the new music was to present rock & roll as a hard-core medium of its own, a radical critique that threatened the stable existence of any established community. The second-generation rockers were self-conscious rebels. Elvis had been a rebel by definition, never by choice; he had no taste for the mass bohemianism that followed Beatlemania. The

Hollywood beckoned: on the sets of *King Creole* (preceding page) and *Jailhouse Rock* (right, with Judy Tyler).

156

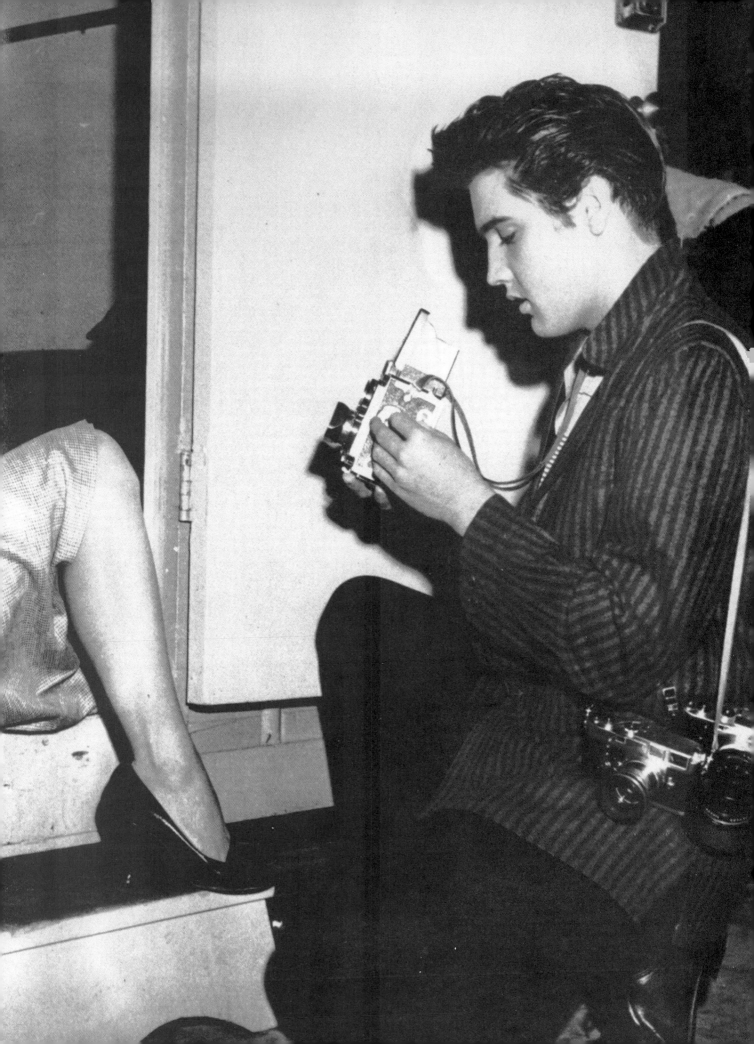

Beatles' long hair, the Stones' dirty sneers, Dylan's polysyllabic verbal obtuseness: All these were a response to things people had seen in Elvis but they had very little to do with how Elvis saw himself. In the end, Elvis was still too big to join forces with any trend or movement; such alliances could only diminish him. Besides, he was far too arrogant to acknowledge that anyone had found a better or more popular approach to music or stardom, much less accept a boost from another performer.

Yet his reputation during these years—when he was buried on the charts, all but ignored, cited by upstart Limeys and hippies not as an example of America realized but of America gone to seed—must have been a burning humiliation to Elvis, whether he ever let it show or not. He was insulated from many things but least of all from his own fame and prosperity.

So he shaped up, changed his act. The adjustments were not sudden nor were they drastic. Fifteen years later, it is barely possible to discern how he made them.

One may pore over the recordings he made between the advent of the Beatles and his own Christmas 1968 television special, and never be quite certain at which moment the Elvis Presley story changed gears. Yet there is little doubt that it did change, and quite some time before that television show was filmed.

Indeed, if one can pinpoint a date, it might be the week of May 25–28, 1966, when Elvis went to RCA's Nashville studios to record the sacred music that eventually became *How Great Thou Art*. This was a significant session for several reasons. It was the first time in twenty-eight months that Elvis had recorded any non-soundtrack music, it was his first Nashville session without Chet Atkins, and it was his first session with a new producer, Felton Jarvis.

It's hard to say just how important Felton Jarvis was to the music Elvis made in the late Sixties. Certainly, Elvis was never one to let his record producer have the upper hand—his passivity was never that simple. Although Elvis never pursued new material, he ultimately determined which songs (of those to which he was exposed) appeared on his records. The most a producer could do was recommend, attempt to

158

get Elvis to pay enough attention so that enough takes of sufficient quality were made and to make certain that the material and the recordings themselves were of acceptable technical quality. Chet Atkins, who had produced all the Presley records for RCA since 1956, was even more passive than Elvis. In the early sessions, it was Presley, not Atkins, who insisted on dozens of takes of songs like "Hound Dog" in order to make certain that he got them right. Later, when Elvis stopped pushing, Atkins let him slide, which makes a kind of sense. Atkins has a considerable reputation as a country guitarist and as a country producer but he was rarely even credited on his Elvis productions, and he had little sympathy with the more blues-based music Elvis sang, so there was no advantage in too much exertion. Atkins, himself an executive in RCA's Nashville operation, was just doing a chore.

Felton Jarvis, on the other hand, was an Elvis fan from way back. In 1959, Jarvis had actually recorded an Elvis tribute record, "Don't Knock Elvis," one of that odd genre of salutes that followed Presley throughout his career. Since then, Jarvis had become a staff producer at ABC-Paramount, where he worked with R&B acts like Lloyd Price, Fats Domino and Gladys Knight and the Pips. Jarvis also produced Tommy Roe's latter-day rockabilly hit, "Sheila," in 1962.

Now, Jarvis was an RCA staff producer; Elvis was one of his first assignments. It was a good match. Jarvis had some ideas about what

Natalie Wood was once a steady friend: in Memphis (left) and with DJ Dewey Phillips (above).

Elvis had been doing wrong, but he also had tremendous respect for Elvis as a singer. The Nashville recording studio and the members of the band did not change, but Jarvis was able to tighten up the recordings technically—to a certain extent, he "professionalized" Elvis' sound.

More importantly, Jarvis was the first insider in a long time who tried to pull Elvis' coat toward more interesting songs. One of the secular songs recorded that May, for instance, was Bob Dylan's "Tomorrow Is a Long Time," in a beautiful version later included on the *Spinout* soundtrack LP.

Unfortunately, Elvis' primary commitment was still to the horrid soundtrack albums. It wasn't until September 1967, a full sixteen months later, that Jarvis was again able to work with Elvis in an extensive non-soundtrack session, but the results were worth the wait. Jarvis was leading Elvis back to the kind of blues and country material he'd recorded at Sun. At those September sessions, he cut Jimmy Reed's "Big Boss Man," Tommy Tucker's "Hi-Heel Sneakers," and Ray Charles' pop-country "You Don't Know Me." The sessions weren't consistently great by any means, but a corner was slowly being turned.

It paid off, too. "Big Boss Man" and "Guitar Man," the country-rock songs written by Nashville session guitarist Jerry Reed, became Elvis' biggest hits since 1966. Apparently, Elvis was pleased, for in January 1968 he returned to the studio for a quick session designed to churn out a new single. He cut only two songs: Chuck Berry's "Too Much Monkey Business," and "U.S. Male," a reprise of "Guitar Man," also written by Reed. It was the first time in memory that Elvis had done an all-rock & roll session, and when "U.S. Male" was released in March, it climbed the charts to Number Twenty-eight, Elvis' deepest invasion of pop music since 1966.

Whether anyone else knew it or not, Elvis was now certain that he could compete with the best again, that he had found his musical focus once more. The changes were subtle, almost too easy. He had re-created the idol, but did not bother to notice that though one foot was pure gold, the other was clay. No matter. The moment had come to announce the King's return.

"He's a great singer. Gosh, he's so great. You have no idea how great he is, really, you don't. You have absolutely no comprehension—it's absolutely impossible. I can't tell you why he's so great, but he is."
—Phil Spector, 1969

In January 1968, Col. Parker and NBC Television's Tom Sarnoff announced plans for an hour-long Christmastime special. This would be Elvis' first television appearance since a 1960 Frank Sinatra special just after his release from the Army. It would also be the first time Elvis had confronted a live audience in seven years.

Hollywood was not stunned. Elvis simply didn't mean much to the film colony. If anything, TV pundits probably wondered why NBC would risk so much ($500,000; an hour of

On the sets of *Flaming Star* (above) and *Blue Hawaii* (right).

prime time) on him. The news didn't make many Elvis fans burst with anticipation either. The hard-core devotees (those who rushed to buy every record and saw all the movies) knew what to expect and, for that matter, so did the more marginal Elvis fans (those who picked and chose among the product but hadn't entirely lost their fascination with the man). Elvis was now a family man: The previous May, he had married his gothic Graceland princess, Priscilla Beaulieu, and on February 1, he would become a father. The new special would be Elvis' coming out as an adult, the rock & roll generation's successor to Perry Como and Andy Williams. As he had on his Steve Allen appearance, thirteen years earlier, Elvis would wear a tuxedo, but this time without the blue suede shoes or any other symbols of rebellion.

That's exactly the special Col. Parker planned. In the Colonel's vision, Elvis appeared onstage, mumbled season's greetings, sang a couple dozen Christmas carols, ballads and novelty numbers, offered another benediction and split.

That is, Elvis would do exactly what any anonymous TV hack would have done, only less of it and for a higher price. This was Parker's dream of holiday bliss.

Parker's dream was producer/director Steve Binder's nightmare. Binder had solid credentials: He had created *The T.A.M.I. Show*, a 1964 concert film featuring everyone from James Brown, the Ronettes and the Rolling Stones to Lesley Gore, the Supremes and Billy J. Kramer and the Dakotas—the perfect document of its rock & roll era. Binder had also directed some episodes of NBC's prime-time rock show, "Hullabaloo," and he ran his production company in partnership with Bones Howe, the best rock engineer in Los Angeles. (Howe had worked on some of the early Presley recordings.)

In short, Binder was just the sort of Elvis fan who had been most disappointed and alienated by Presley's failures of nerve and quality. To Binder, the NBC show would be Elvis' moment of truth. If he did another MGM movie on the special, he could wipe out his career and he

The Beatles presented the first serious challenge to Presley's reign. Here, Elvis inspects a German magazine featuring the Fab Four in early 1964.

would be known only as that phenomenon who came along in the Fifties, shook his hips and had a great manager. On the reverse side, if he could do a special and prove that he was still Number One, he could have a whole rejuvenation thing going.

Maybe. Elvis wasn't in the best of shape commercially, but he had begun to make the musical adaptations that led to his creative rehabilitation when he recorded "Guitar Man" and "U.S. Male," the previous autumn, long before he ever met Binder. Those songs hit the charts, the most successful records Elvis had had in years, just as Binder began preproduction, early in 1968. Together, "Guitar Man" and "U.S. Male" reestablished rock & roll as the foundation of Elvis' appeal, an impression reinforced by the fact that all of the nonrock singles that followed them flopped badly. By mid-1968, that is, Elvis was already well on his way to a musical resurgence. His audience was once more demanding blues and rock & roll from him, and Elvis was not only unable to deny the audience for very long, he was also still a great rock and blues singer.

The TV special, then, was an opportunity for an elaborate and dramatic announcement and confirmation of Presley's continuing genius. It was not automatically a high artistic risk because even marginal fans would have to tune in for one last glimpse of the King, one last chance for him to reign again. If there was a problem, it was making Elvis aware of how high the stakes could be. Only Elvis, on the other hand, could raise the pot to its limit.

To put it plainly, Steve Binder wasn't the guiding genius behind Elvis in 1968 any more than Sam Phillips had been in 1954 or Col. Parker had been in 1958: What carried the show was Elvis and his music, which transcended every obstacle it faced, every shred of mediocrity. Steve Binder has never again produced another show of the quality of the Elvis special—for that matter, most of the production, staging and choreography of the Elvis special itself was sheer formula television.

Binder did play a crucial role in the special: He filled a spot that had been too long missing from Presley's creative environment. He was the instigator, the man who pushed Elvis to the

On the *Girls, Girls, Girls* set, with Scatter, Elvis' pet chimp.

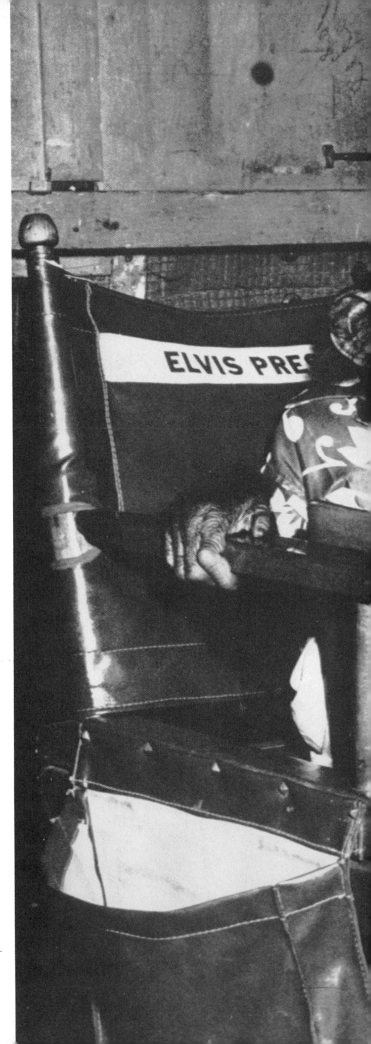

hilt, forcing him to use the deepest and best parts of himself, inciting Elvis to work hard for once, to lay aside his laziness and *prove* that he was as great as his myth said he was.

First, Binder had to convince Elvis that his prowess was in doubt. So, the most important moment in the "comeback" special came that afternoon during preproduction when Binder suggested that Elvis and the Memphis Mafiosi take a stroll on the Sunset Strip sidewalk outside Binder's office, just to test the reaction to an unannounced, relatively unguarded appearance by the King. Elvis was undoubtedly wary —he hadn't dared such a daylight visit to a public streetcorner in a decade—but he agreed to the test.

So, for perhaps ten or fifteen minutes, Elvis loitered outside a topless bar. Pedestrians strolled on by in the midday heat. Incredulous, Elvis began to cut up, trying to call attention to himself. As time passed, his antics became less and less subtle. Nothing worked. Chastened, he returned to Binder's office.

Now, it must be admitted that pedestrians in Southern California are atypical; this is not the land of foot traffic. Furthermore, the pedestrians of Sunset Strip in the psychedelic haze of 1968 were pretty strange, even for California pedestrians. In fact, one certain way to be ignored on Sunset Strip, no matter how much you resemble a celebrity, is to attempt to call attention to yourself. The blasé population won't flinch as a matter of principle.

This made the experiment something of a set-up, since Binder surely knew that the most un-hip thing imaginable on the Strip was to react to the presence of a star. It's hard to believe that Elvis would have met similar apathy on a corner in Fayetteville, Chattanooga or Fresno.

Elvis had been isolated for too long, and he was too confused by his drop in record sales and movie grosses to consider the reaction on the Strip anything but a symptom. This was a more profound threat to him than any drop in revenues. His career might stagnate but, despite all his economic insecurity, Elvis knew he would never have to return to the poverty of his youth. The withering of his notoriety, on the other hand, was something he could not stand.

If Elvis possessed a single uncomplicated goal in life, it was to become an unignorable man. If he had a straightforward, easily explainable reason for his long hair, his pink shirts and flashy suits, for his Cadillacs and mansions and the huge rings now adorning his fingers, it was his unquenchable desire for recognition. He could not bear the thought of anonymity.

Elvis used the special as an immediate vehicle to escape such a fate. He was willing to allow an unprecedented probing into his private life, as Binder filmed several hours of reminiscences among himself and the Memphis Mafia (not that anything was revealed); he was willing to work more freely than ever before with writers, arrangers, producers and directors from outside his tight cocoon of cronies and security flunkies; he was willing to have his tastes and instincts challenged. In the end, he was even willing to buck the bosses for once in his life.

Binder insisted that the special could not be a Christmas program. Col. Parker insisted that it

Love me tender: on the movie set (above) and on the S.S. *Matsonia* (left). Overleaf: 3764 Highway 51 South, Memphis, a.k.a. Graceland.

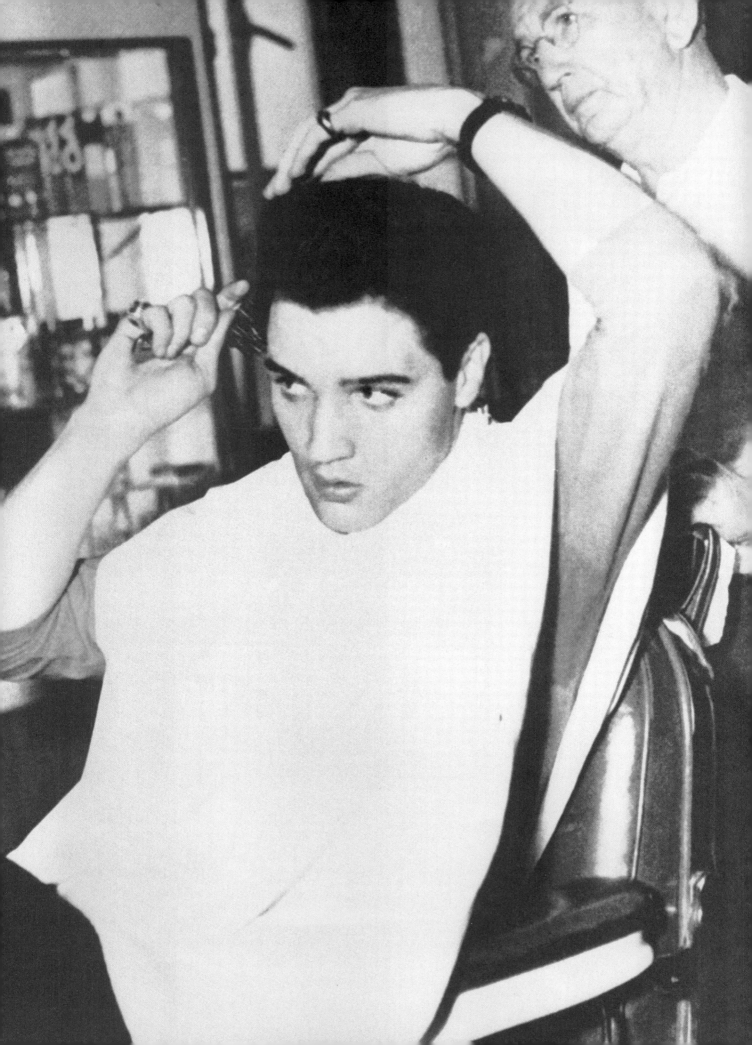

must be. Elvis would not confront the Colonel directly—he still yessed him on every point—but when the Colonel left the room, Elvis assured Binder that everything would be all right, and he cooperated fully in subverting Parker's plans for Pablum-ized music and production.

Binder got more than just this cooperation when he suggested that stroll on the Strip. In fact, he might have got this much anyway since Elvis had come into the special knowing that he

In between films in the Sixties: touch football with the Memphis Mafia.

needed a new approach. What Binder got that afternoon on the block was bigger and better than mere cooperation: He got an Elvis Presley who was determined, once again, to go out there and *show 'em*.

Binder's original concept for the special centered on a plot in which an innocent young man first encounters the world and its wickedness. It wasn't all that far from the hackneyed melodrama of the Elvis movie but Binder wanted to do this story more boldly, with an element of the risqué. Rather than place the Elvis character among whitewashed carny folk or scrubbed-up stock drivers, Binder wanted to put him down amid the hustlers on a honky-tonk strip, Beale Street gone Vegas.

In the opening scene, the character entered a brothel. Though no action took place, and a judge as astute as Phil Spector would later claim that the brothel sequence was the best thing in the whole special, the NBC censors forbade showing it. As a result, the story line (which had always been tenuous) was scrapped. In the final tape, only a segment featuring Elvis confronting the highest roller on the strip, set to Jimmy Reed's "Big Boss Man," survives.

Just as well. All fictionalized poor-boy stories pale alongside the reality of Elvis in the flesh—that was one reason the Elvis films were doomed. Without interference from a story line, Elvis simply shaped the special around himself. Although some of the staging is unbelievably hokey (particularly the deracinated dance sequence built around "Motherless Child," which is the antithesis of the gospel music Elvis loved), for the most part, Elvis simply stripped away all pretense. He was presenting a man-monument, a candidate for Mt. Rushmore. He was enacting the living legend, a tribute to his own glory.

He had prepared for this moment. Elvis was slender, more slender than he had been even in the Fifties; he had the cheekbones of a god and the tan that went with them. Dressed in a tight black leather suit, his hair slicked back at the sides, with just a suggestion of a waterfall in front, he was not only the Elvis of everyone's dreams, he was actually a little bit better: He

was that boy who had climbed on the mystery train and returned home as an adult, ready to tell tales and spin yarns of adventure. And he had that gaze in his eyes again, the one that said he was ready to conquer the universe, perish the cost. Elvis Presley was a singularly handsome man for most of his years but on the comeback special he was radiant, a great American beauty, the idealized Everyman come to life.

The special opened in stark simplicity. A blue neon logo spells out E-L-V-I-S across a black screen. After a few seconds, the words *Singer Presents* appear above it. There is no announcer. But as the logo fades and the band kicks in, we hear a voice:

Lookin' for trouble?
You came to the right place.
Lookin' for trouble?
Then look right in my face.
I was born standin' up,
    and talkin' back
My daddy was a green-eyed mountain jack.

As he sings these lines, hammered out with

Above: with friend Dorothy Harmony.

176

bludgeoning power, recited to a Bo Diddley beat, Elvis' face fills the screen—by the end of the first verse, the camera has pulled back and there he is, all of him, for the first time in years. It's an awesome moment, and as Elvis swings into "Guitar Man" he is duplicated on a giant backdrop, where his name is again spelled in neon, this time saturated red, with a hundred guitar-playing dancers atop it, around it, even inside it. This is something more than a gesture —it is a demonstration of Elvis' conviction of his universality, his stature as the embodiment of American multiplicity. It is an unbelievably arrogant moment and, when fully realized, it no longer matters whose idea any bit of staging may have been because Elvis possesses all of it. In that moment, Presley is like Melville's whale in the first moment that we see him, glimpsed not in terror but in awe. And, like Melville's, the genius of Elvis is such that this moment is suspended, its tone held throughout the show, so that every second Elvis is on the screen, we feel how special and precious he is.

"There is something magical about watching a man who has lost himself find his way back home," wrote Jon Landau. "He sang with the kind of power people no longer expect from rock 'n' roll singers. He moved his body with a lack of pretension and effort that must have made Jim Morrison green with envy. And while most of the songs were ten or twelve years old, he performed them as freshly as though they were written yesterday."

In a way, those songs *were* completely fresh because Elvis sang them with so much purity and intelligence, humor and nonchalance, intensity and purpose, so much vigor and so much restraint. The age of "Jailhouse Rock" or "Guitar Man," "Love Me Tender" or "Trouble" mattered no more than the age of "Milkcow Blues Boogie" or "Baby, Let's Play House" had mattered on those long-ago nights in Memphis.

Elvis spent part of the program onstage, appearing before a live audience, surrounded by cronies (including Scotty Moore and D. J. Fontana). He was supposed to reminisce, tell a few stories about the old days, catalogue his reactions to the changes in music, reveal himself at last. That was Steve Binder's vision, not Elvis'. He remained almost as mute as ever, passing over all the issues of his life, his career, his im-

pact, with a shrug and a homily. He would not speak his mind.

Where he showed himself was in the music, as much as he ever had—which means that he showed himself completely. He showed his ambition, and he showed how much of what he'd set out to accomplish had been realized, and he revealed the majesty he had discovered along the way. He sang old songs, but he sang them so differently it was hard to recall ever hearing them before.

There was a technical reason, of course. Elvis' vocal range had lowered considerably with the years; his tones had literally mellowed, so that he no longer had the high, lonesome ache of his Sun days. But that high voice had been replaced by a new one that was totally assured, that did not ask questions so much as it confronted mysteries. Especially, Elvis now sang ballads with total command.

On the *Blue Hawaii* soundtrack, "Can't Help Falling in Love" stands out as a gem among dross. But on the TV show, Elvis did something more with the song: He sang it as if he had taken the measure of every syllable. And more than that, Elvis sang as if he were, for the first time, realizing that this song, above all others, described his relationship with his audience. "Shall I stay?" he crooned. "Would it be a sin? If I can't help falling in love with you." What he knew—and what no one hearing him could fail to know—was that those words really described the way Elvis fans saw Elvis: as a figure of fate, the inevitable, unavoidable man. And he knew it was true; he really was that man. In such moments, one understood why such an insecure man had become a singer and a hero.

With the special, Elvis had finally found a vehicle that claimed his place in the world. Rather than being put in his place, he was, for once, taking what was his by right. You could hear his assurance, over and over, repeated in the hottest version of "Lawdy, Miss Clawdy" ever recorded and in the way he mocked the lyrics of "Love Me Tender." Most of all, you could hear it when he turned Col. Parker's obligatory Christmas number into the bluest "Blue Christmas" in history and then followed it with a version of "One Night" that began as a joke and wound up as an act of defiance, inserting the lines—"The things we did and saw/

In 1960 Vernon married Dee Stanley. Here, the family at the Memphis Airport, en route to Hollywood; a very young Priscilla is at lower left, with various Memphis Mafia members and fans in the background.

Would make the earth stand still''—which had been denied him a decade earlier. And as he cut through that nasty blues on TV for the world to see and hear, everyone knew and believed. This was not a king regaining his throne; this was a king asserting his right to rule.

Throughout the production, Binder and Parker had been in near-continuous conflict. The producer had very specific ideas about how Elvis had to change to appeal to a contemporary audience; the Colonel wasn't interested, especially since many of Binder's ideas involved awakening Elvis' awareness of his own abilities again. It had been touchy enough to lull Elvis into acquiescence when he was a vulnerable hillbilly kid. Managing a reinvigorated thirty-three-year-old independently wealthy man was not what Parker had in mind.

Everything came to a head in the controversy over the show's finale. Parker insisted on closing with a Christmas song; Binder insisted on an original song and, more than that, an original message song, one that would leave viewers with a sense that Elvis had made a statement of how much he cared.

For days, Parker and Binder bickered back and forth. Finally, Binder simply defied the Colonel and commissioned the special's choral director, Earl Brown, to write a song. The next day, Brown played it for Elvis on the piano. Elvis asked to hear it again and again, about a half-dozen times altogether. Then he simply said he'd do it. (The Colonel kept up his threats until Brown agreed to cut Hill and Range, via the Presley companies, in on the publishing action.)

The song Brown wrote was called "If I Can Dream." It was close to being a hymn, and the pop-soul arrangement Howe found for it was perfect, grounded in Larry Knectal's pulsing bass and Don Randi's ecclesiastical organ. The words verged on sentimental corn, but Elvis delivered them with such raw conviction that the impulse behind them came clear. What Brown had done, in effect, was write a song that described Elvis' vision of his own life. If Binder wanted revelation, this was as close as Elvis could come to giving it to him.

In the finished program, "If I Can Dream" is a kind of epilogue. The black-leathered Elvis

---

Behind the scenes at Graceland: the pink Cadillac is at right.

leaves the stage, the screen fades to black and then Elvis returns, this time dressed in a pure white three-piece suit, like a cross between the shrewdest gambler on the river and a carny-hip Baptist preacher. Behind him the giant red neon ELVIS looms again. Elvis looks down, as if meditating, then straight at the camera as he sings, softly, carefully, measuring the words:

*There must be lights/Burnin' brighter
Somewhere.
Got to be birds, flyin' higher/In a sky
More blue.*

Elvis simply bears down until he reaches the final lines, which are the ones that best tell his story. He sings them with the camera tight on his face, until the very end:

*Deep in my heart/There's a tremblin'
Question.
Still I am sure that the answer, answer's
gonna come/Somehow.
Out there in the dark—there's a beckoning candle
And while I can think, while I can talk,
While I can stand, while I can walk,
While I can dream
Please, let my dream/Come true
Right now!*

It was corny. It was show biz. It was Elvis.

RCA released "If I Can Dream" as a single in late October, six weeks in advance of the special's air date. But the song didn't creep into *Billboard*'s Hot 100 until the end of November. A week later, after the special was shown, the record exploded. By January, it reached Number Twelve, Elvis' biggest single since "I'm Yours" in 1965. The soundtrack album from the special, *Elvis*, reached Number Eight. Presley was reestablished as an important recording artist.

Elvis' musical confidence had been regained but he remained tied to old contracts. Between the completion of the special and the end of 1969, three more feature films were released. *Charro!*, released in March 1969, was Elvis' only purely dramatic movie—he doesn't have a single musical scene in the picture. But *Charro!* is a downbeat Western, released at a time when even the best Westerns were finding it hard to discover an audience. (And *Charro!* was not one

of the best Westerns of this or any period.) *The Trouble with Girls (And How to Get into It)* returned Elvis to familiar musical-comedy territory—it was typically humdrum. But the final fictional feature of his motion-picture career, *Change of Habit*, was a different story, perhaps because it wasn't shot until midway through 1969. By then Elvis was in the midst of one of his most creative periods.

In the chronology of Elvis' career, 1969 ranks in importance alongside 1954, 1955 and 1956. This was the year in which Elvis reached his musical maturity. In 1969 he made the most sophisticated recordings of his career, appeared in one of his few truly interesting films and topped it off with a thunderous return to the stage in Las Vegas. Yet, like all of Elvis' moments of greatest success, 1969 also contained seeds of disaster.

The year's work began in mid-January, with a ten-day session at American Recording in Memphis, the first time Elvis had recorded in his hometown since leaving Sun for RCA. American Recording was on a tremendous hot streak,

Awards for all occasions. Early recognition from RCA (left) and sharing the stage at an awards ceremony with Billy Fury (above).

fast becoming the most successful independent recording studio in the country. Producer/engineer Chips Moman, one of the owners, was in the midst of a twenty-eight-month hot streak in which he worked on ninety-seven chart records. American's biggest successes were the Box Tops ("Cry Like a Baby," "The Letter," "Soul Deep"); Jerry Wexler of Atlantic also recorded the great Dusty Springfield album, *Dusty in Memphis*, as well as some Wilson Pickett sides, at American during this period.

The attraction of the studio was primarily the house band led by bassist Tommy Cogbill. All of these players were younger than the musicians Elvis worked with in Nashville. Cogbill's band was full of white Southerners who had been inspired to begin playing by Elvis; like the musicians in Muscle Shoals, Alabama, and across town at Stax, they were the direct heirs of his Sun synthesis. What they played went by several names—blue-eyed soul, swamp pop— but it was inevitably a product of the same cir-

The Memphis Mafia team graduated from informal football games to uniformed matches. Left: in L.A., the early Sixties.

cumstances and impulses as Elvis' music. When Elvis entered American Recording, he'd come home in more ways than one.

Presley had connections to a few of the players. Guitarist Reggie Young and organist Bobby Emmons played with Bill Black's Combo after the late Black had left Elvis; drummer Gene Christman had been in Jerry Lee Lewis' band for a time. But the real link was soul, a shared feeling for blues that transcended race.

Elvis booked American for ten days in mid-January but he was able to work for only six of them, after coming down with laryngitis. Yet in less than a week, Elvis and the American house band cut three Top Ten singles ("In the Ghetto," "Suspicious Minds," "Don't Cry Daddy") as well as a number of outstanding album tracks ("Long Black Limousine," "Wearin' That Loved On Look," "I'm Movin' On"). Recorded far more clearly and cleanly than any of Elvis' Nashville or Hollywood sides, these thirty-six tracks are genuine pop records, not just a bunch of songs slapped down on tape.

When he returned to American in February for an additional five days of recording, Elvis laid down another hit single, "Kentucky Rain," and another batch of fine album tracks as well: "Only the Strong Survive," "Stranger in My Own Home Town," "It Keeps Right On A-Hurtin'."

The albums that emerged from these sessions, *From Elvis in Memphis* and the studio disc of the *From Memphis to Vegas/From Vegas to Memphis* set, are the first truly adult records of Elvis' career. They are thematically mature

and musically sophisticated; rather than simply being layered on, the strings, horns and backing voices are fully integrated into the arrangements. Their diversity is outstanding. The songs range from contemporary soul hits to country standards, with a batch of the best new songs Elvis had ever been given. Hill and Range had now lost some of its grip on Elvis' career, as a result of its inability to deliver hits in the past few years; maintaining absolute control would have been pointless and self-destructive. Although Elvis would always record some mediocre slop as a concession to the publishers, their trash would no longer be the bulk of his material.

Very little of what Elvis recorded in Memphis is rock & roll; none of it is straight blues. Yet all of the tracks derive their sense of aggression from rock, and their groove is inevitably born of the blues. The very best tracks are quite beyond genre: "Wearin' That Loved On Look," the Dallas Frazier song that kicks off *From Elvis in Memphis*, begins with a gospel growl from Elvis, picks up a churchy organ, blues-rock guitar, show-band percussion and soul chorus but the heart of the lyric is a country saga of infidelity.

The Memphis singles reestablished Elvis as a Top Ten hitmaker. "In the Ghetto," released in May, is as close as Presley ever came to a protest record, and if the lyric is finally far too sentimental, it must be remembered how radical a departure it was for such a true Son of the South as Elvis to record colorblind material, even in 1969. Besides, Elvis needed some more committed material to follow up "If I Can Dream," for credibility's sake, if for no other reason. A third vaguely socially oriented single, "Clean Up Your Own Backyard" barely scraped into the Top Forty, but this time Elvis switched gears smoothly, rebounding with the best of all the American tracks, "Suspicious Minds."

"Suspicious Minds" is the archetype and the apex of all of Elvis' late-Sixties music. It was the last Number One single of his career, and it earned its stature, for it was also by far the most well-crafted single he ever made.

In structure, "Suspicious Minds" is deceptively simple. Led by a propulsive bass line, the

With Lou Costello, Ferlin Husky and Jane Russell in Las Vegas (left) and clowning with fans in L.A. (right).

record at first seems to boil down to Elvis and a choir of female voices. But what's really going on is seamless modern record-making—this is the first and just about the only Elvis record that could truly be described as "produced"—in which strings, brass, the odd saxophone, guitar line and drums intermingle effortlessly, a marvel of technology. At the end, as his voice and the chorus, the bass and the brass, the strings and the percussion rise in a seemingly endless crescendo, Elvis is not simply working at the peak of his form: He has reached a level of exaltation he hadn't known since the boat left for West Germany.

"Suspicious Minds" was followed by two similar, if ultimately slighter, hits, the bathetic "Don't Cry Daddy" and the gorgeously paranoiac "Kentucky Rain." The Memphis albums are cut from the same cloth. *From Elvis in Memphis* is almost the only conceptually and stylistically coherent album Elvis ever made. *From Memphis to Vegas/From Vegas to Memphis* (later released separately as *Elvis in Person at the International Hotel, Las Vegas, Nevada* and *Back in Memphis*) isn't quite as strong, partly because the studio music had already been picked over for the first album and partly because of the disparity between making great records and giving a great show. This gap was to plague Elvis for the next decade, as more and more records of his concert music were released.

Elvis had been kept off the stage for nearly a decade because Col. Parker hadn't been able to conceive of a way to make concerts as profitable as movies. But Presley was so turned on by the two shows he gave in the course of making the TV special, and his film grosses had so badly deteriorated that Parker had little choice but to explore the possibility of doing live performances. The question was how to maximize the profits.

Initially, the Colonel decided that the answer was to play huge stadiums; he wanted to earn at least $100,000 per night—something he didn't consider possible playing indoors. Then came the opportunity to play the vast new International Hotel in Las Vegas, the biggest and glitziest joint in town. The price was right: a million dollars for two weeks, two shows a night. This was less than Parker could have earned from twenty-eight stadium gigs (if they could have

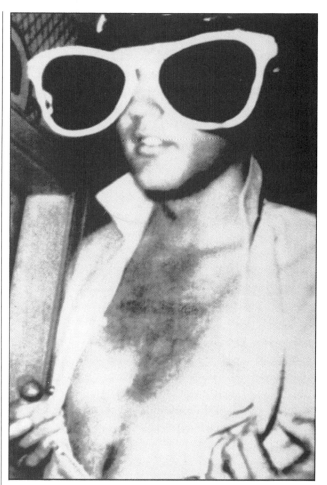

found that many), but expenses would be minimal (no travel; in Vegas tradition, a substantial share of hotel and meal charges are picked up by the house).

The location was perfect for another reason. Col. Parker was an inveterate high roller, the kind of gambler for whom casinos are kept open around the clock. The chance to spend two weeks in Vegas on business wasn't something Parker could afford to pass up.

Elvis didn't have such high expectations. He remembered his disastrous 1956 appearance at the Frontier. He was confronted with returning to the stage in the full glare of the national media after a nine-year absence, with a show that had been rehearsed, but had never been played before a live audience, with no time at all to work out the kinks. There was no reason to suppose—or, anyway, no way to discover—whether the Vegas audience of 1969 would be any more sympathetic than the Vegas crowd of 1956.

Still, Elvis continued to follow orders. In July, he went to Los Angeles to assemble a band

Taking Care of Business: some of the Memphis Mafia in the mid-Sixties (left to right), Joe Esposito, unknown, Bullets Durgom, the Colonel, Mrs. Parker, the King, Larry Geller, George Klein, Alan Fortas, Marty Lacker and Richard Davis. They all had jobs on the movie set.

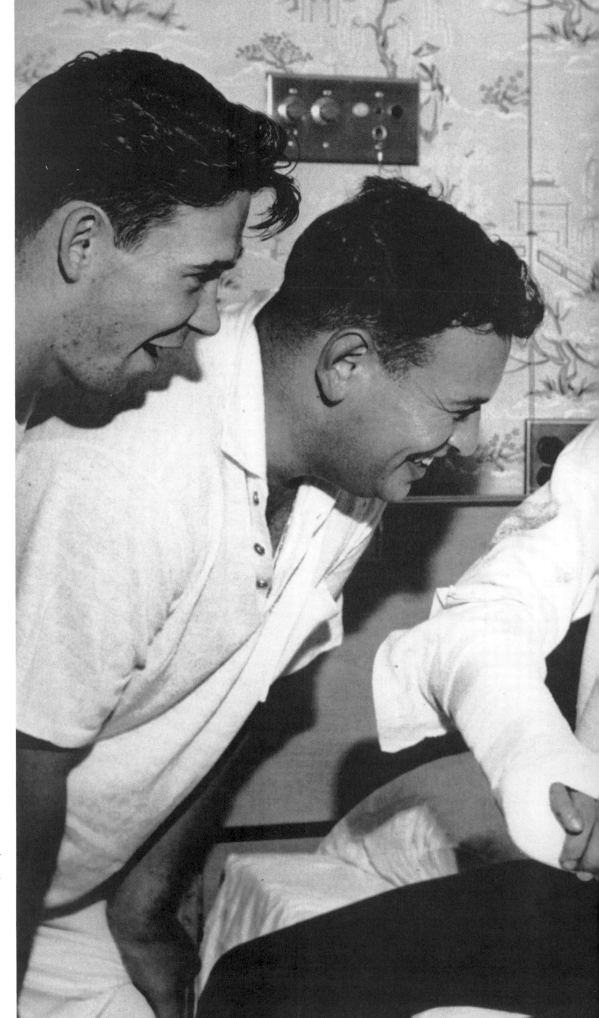

Elvis surrounded by his Mafia;
he had broken his finger playing
touch football with the team.
Following pages: Elvis is more
successful as a water skiier, here
with Sonny Neal, Bob Neal's
son, on McKellar Lake in
Memphis.

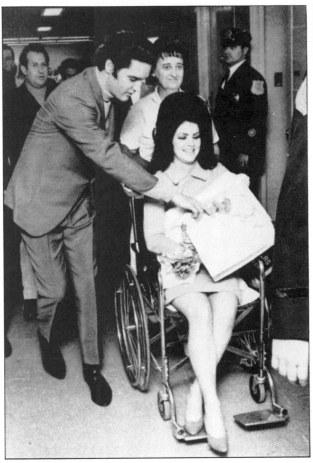

and begin rehearsals. He put together a fine band: Led by guitarist James Burton, featuring drummer Ronnie Tutt, the personnel of this group would change very little over the next eight years.

There was no reason to change it; this was just about Elvis' dream group, led by a red-hot Southern blues guitarist (Burton had become a star in 1957, at age fifteen, by playing on Dale Hawkins' "Suzie Q") and a drummer who played with rock & roll power but with a big-band sense of swing. Together with bassist Jerry Scheff, keyboard player Larry Muhoberac and guitarists/vocalists John Wilkinson and Charlie Hodge, they rehearsed for a month and turned up in Vegas with the most successful show the town had ever seen.

It was a mixture of comedy and rock & roll, gospel music and pop ballads, third-rate jokes and first-class songs, a blend of genius, trivia and self-abnegation, arrogance, laziness and charm. It was fundamentally Southern, and it was even more fundamentally American. It was the ultimate success story, with a promise of more to come. Had it closed with "When You

Wish upon a Star," its perfection could not have been more complete.

Yet Elvis remained doubtful of his reception —the old scars ran deep. Opening dignitaries included Pat Boone and Fats Domino, folk-singer Phil Ochs and soundtrack maestro Henry Mancini. Which were on his side?

Elvis made sure his own were with him. He even called Sam Phillips in Memphis, to make sure he would be there and, of course, Sam was. Even then his fears persisted. "Elvis was clearly unsure of himself, worried that he wouldn't get through to people after all those years, and re-lieved and happy when he realized we were with him," wrote Ellen Willis in *The New Yorker*.

Willis also picked up on the progress Elvis made, how quickly he adjusted to the mood people brought to his show, ". . . the next night he was loose enough to fool around with the audience," she continued, "accepting handker-chiefs to mop his forehead and reaching out his hands to women in the front row. During both performances there was a fair amount of sighing and screaming, but like Elvis' sexual posturing, it was more in fun than in ecstasy. It was the ritual that counted . . ."

That's it, exactly, the summation of Elvis' career from that day forward. Having con-quered Vegas, television and radio a second time, he had established himself as King in more ways than one. Elvis was now unstoppa-ble, untoppable and well aware of it. He was, not to put too fine a point on it, in the clear again, and this time, not as a rebel but as a con-queror. The years of fame and fatness had taken their toll and Elvis was not liable to run any unnecessary risks ever again. So he per-fected his Vegas show and took it out on the road for concert tours, took it back to Vegas a couple times a year, for fine tuning. But basi-cally, it remained what it was on the night Wil-lis saw it: a ritual, with Elvis as priest and Host all at once.

He wore splendiferous raiment, costumes of multirhinestone complexity or simple cotton karate ghees. He could thunder into heavy, big-band rock & roll arrangements or sing relaxed pop ballads. He might sing with full-throttle

Elvis married Priscilla on May 1, 1967, at the Alladin Hotel, Las Vegas. Above: leaving the hospital with baby Lisa Marie, born February 1, 1968. Right: all's well at Graceland.

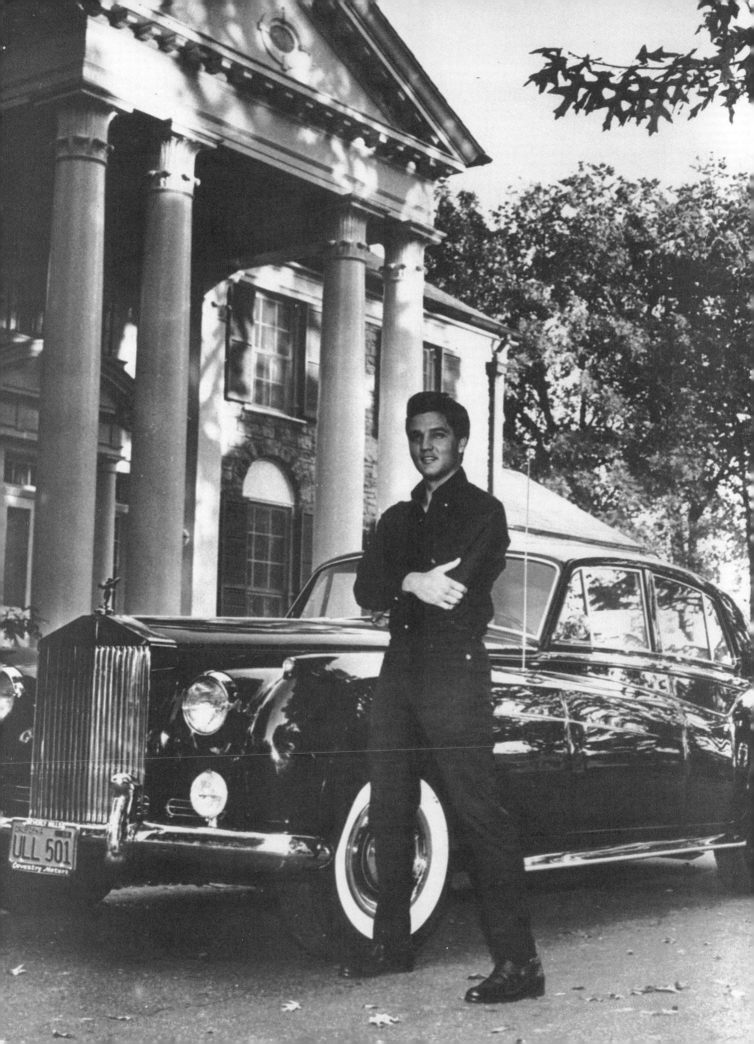

He had not succumbed to his myth so much as he had vanished into his own mythology. And whether this meant that he was trapped or liberated no one was ever certain, until it was too late to make any difference.

What counted, his performances said firmly, was the great ceremony alone. All that mattered was the drama of this innocent boy who became emperor of all he surveyed. He was the ultimate symbol of what Leslie Fiedler called "the dream of innocence and the fact of guilt."

Inevitably, Elvis lost track of himself, becoming so wrapped up in his glorious depiction of his glorious self that he came to believe in it. His belief was not without irony and humor but it was belief nonetheless.

The extent of this conviction is revealed in the final scenes of *Change of Habit*, his last dramatic movie. What a perfectly appropriate title this was to end the chapter of the tale entitled *Elvis in Hollywood*, and how poorly received.

The plot is no more plausible than any of the other Elvis vehicles. Indeed, with its casting of Elvis as a ghetto doctor, an urban Schweitzer, *Change of Habit* may have been the most surreal Presley plot of all. Yet this was the time of "If I Can Dream" and "In the Ghetto." As mawkish as they may be, the scenes in which Elvis works to heal are also affecting, if only because they clue us in to the other side of his ambition, the generosity, not the greed. The scenes in which Elvis becomes a faith healer, cuddling a tiny, mute girl and crooning "love you" over and over, are virtually unwatchable, but they are also in keeping with his vision of himself. As is the center of the plot, which involves Mary Tyler Moore as a nun in mufti who has fallen in love with Elvis (who also falls for her).

In the end, Mary goes back to the convent, unable to decide between Elvis and God. Elvis tails her there and in order to ease the decision, picks up his guitar and leads a folk-rock mass. Mary watches no more decisively than before, wavering with every glance. The camera follows her eyes around the chapel, from icons of Jesus to Elvis in the flesh, singing his gospel-rocker. Back and forth the images flit: Jesus, Elvis, Mary on tenterhooks, Jesus, Elvis.

The purpose of this juxtaposition is not to show us Mary's dilemma more clearly, much less to clarify Mary's ultimate choice. The final

urgency for fifteen minutes or merely sip water and reminisce for an equal spell. He would spin out numberless medleys of old hits, everything from "Mystery Train" to "In the Ghetto," or simply cruise through the most appealing (to him) hits of the day. None of it cost him much.

As Elvis saw it, his job had become very simple: to enact not just the legend of Elvis, but the legend sufficiently emptied of content, so that no person's fantasies were threatened or denied —even though this also meant that no one's fantasies (including Elvis' own) were ever fulfilled. As a gesture, it was awesome in the magnitude of its generosity, an insoluble mixture of humility and conceit. By enacting his legend in two dimensions, Elvis confirmed all suspicions, justified all expectations. It became as easy to see him as the master ripoff artist as it was to envision him as the great American musical genius—or even a genius of America incarnate.

None of this seemed to concern Elvis at all.

Backstage at the 1968 TV special (above) that put Elvis back on the throne. Following pages: the pink Cadillac, permanently parked at Graceland, while Elvis hits the road.

shots of *Change of Habit* are perhaps the most hubristic in all of cinema, for they exist solely to make an equation between Elvis and Christ himself.

That is, *Change of Habit* baldly delivers the message that the rest of Elvis' career attempted to put across with slightly more subtlety. The message is that Elvis can save, that he is a redeemer, that when he picks up his guitar and begins to sing, he is truly bigger than life, though he may move in mysterious ways.

It is ridiculous to worship him, of course. Yet it is quite understandable that, in lieu of making great leaps of faith themselves, many will do just that. And for every innocent American who has ever wondered how a people might find itself bending the knee to monarchy, Elvis and his ceremony offer an answer.

"He was not primitive, like people think. He was an artist, and he was into being an artist. Of course, he was also into rockin' his ass off, but that was part of it. Onstage, he encompassed everything—he was laughing at the world and he was laughing at himself, but at the same time, he was dead serious. . . . It was horrible, and at the same time, it was fantastic."
—*Bruce Springsteen, 1977*

Throughout the Seventies, Elvis enacted his ceremony, and everywhere he went he was received not as an entertainer but as a regent.

Yet no one could help noticing that Elvis had largely lost interest in his ritual. As time went on, his performances became more and more perfunctory and even on those occasions when some exceptional effort was necessary—his New York City debut at Madison Square Garden in 1972, his around-the-world live broadcast from Hawaii in 1973—Elvis was distracted and flabby.

After 1969, there was no chance that Elvis would ever again stand on a streetcorner in anonymity. He was a revered household word now, and if he remained disreputable to the intelligentsia, it was of little consequence to him, since such people were basically foreigners in his world anyhow. Having conquered America and its media not once but twice, Elvis was acceptable and even beloved, a hero to everyone who counted. Never again would he belong among the despised (although the despised might feel that he belonged very much to them); neither was any door closed to him. On a moment's notice, Elvis could see the president of the United States. Once, on a whim, Elvis decided to become a federal narcotics agent; he cut the red tape by going to Richard M. Nixon himself, and Nixon instantly obliged him. It didn't even matter that the president was the only authenticated criminal ever to hold that office or that Elvis himself was one of the worst abusers of prescription drugs in medical history. This was a ritual neither Nixon nor Presley could avoid as they lived out the poor-boy-makes-good legend they had to fulfill.

The fact is, Elvis was bored and lonely. The loneliness was unavoidable—he'd lived with it for twenty years—but the boredom was unbearable: He couldn't stand it for twenty minutes. Neither the Memphis Mafia nor legions of women, buckets of pills, realms of land and fleets of cars could relieve him of it. Once Elvis knew for certain how passionately he was loved, and by how many, he had no goals left. He *had* shown 'em, but in the process he'd trapped himself. Now, he was sealed off from any other avenues of growth.

This was so not because there was nothing left for Elvis to gain but because there was so little to lose. If Elvis could never again fall back into anonymity, if he had proved himself beyond epithets like "white trash," if he was now an American prince, truly King of Rock & Roll, why bother?

So he entered upon his campaign of self-destruction. He gorged himself on all manner of Southern-fried cholesterol (to read the recipes

201

Elvis and Priscilla (left) on their
honeymoon in 1967, and (right)
outside the divorce court in
1973. Following pages: in the
mid-Seventies Elvis gained
weight and took to flamboyant
costumes. Here, at the 1975
Nassau Coliseum concert in
New York, he hands one of his
scarves to a fan.

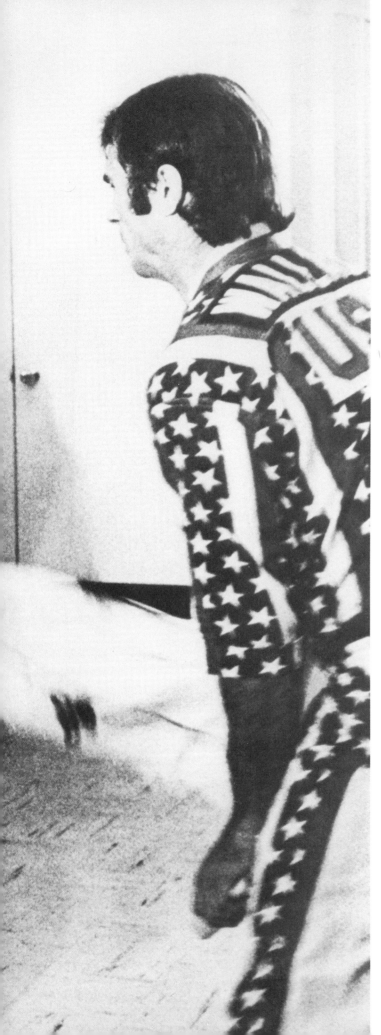

compiled by the Graceland cook is to cease to wonder at his girth), benumbed and overexcited himself with every variety of pill, indulged in ridiculous sleeping marathons. It was as if Elvis had decided that since he was archetypal in one respect, he was obliged to take all that he did to its extreme.

He dabbled in spurious spirituality and cops-and-robbers fantasy, played tyrannical boss one day and gave away cars (and, from time to time, whole houses) the next. In the morning, he might mourn his lost loves, Gladys and Priscilla, but in the evening he would frolic with whores. Elvis swathed himself in jewels and lived in mansions yet he never allowed anyone (let alone himself) to forget his poor-boy beginnings. He squandered it all—fame and fortune, beauty and mental agility, his glorious talent and his marvelous sexuality. There was no particular reason for this. He just did these things because he could. There was no one to stop him, no one even to challenge him. He had not a friend in the world, which is all the incentive most people need to destroy themselves.

He had real problems—back and stomach and eye pains, the anxiety of investment advice that was beginning to sour, and most of all, a

Karate with Red West (above); instructor (left); on stage (overleaf).

touring and performance schedule that was nonsensical and debilitating. Elvis did two shows a night in Las Vegas for years because Col. Parker was either not shrewd enough to negotiate a better deal or had so many conflicts of interest that he did not dare renegotiate. But, in the end, you have to say Elvis became a monster because he had some of that in him, and there was nothing to prevent its full expression.

Does the monstrosity of Elvis really matter? He remained a great artist, and the way he sang contains more "truth" than all the demeaning facts that have festered since his death. Depraved as he may have been, Elvis made outstanding music, both in the studio and in concert, to the very end of his days.

It's even easier to miss the greatness of Elvis' Seventies music than of his despised Sixties sides, in part because so much of what he did was live (and barely reflected, let alone captured, on his live albums). Yet, even sticking solely to studio recordings, during this period Elvis made more than a dozen songs that will survive, though even these are buried amidst tons of dross.

RCA kept Elvis on the same record-releasing schedule they'd begun twenty years earlier, re-

Elvis on the run: in Philadelphia (left) and on his private jet, the *Lisa Marie* (above and overleaf). TCB was the Mafia's motto.

217

leasing three albums plus four or five singles per year. The fundamental difference was that live recordings and the occasional repackaging of old material replaced the movie soundtracks as the bulk of his releases. In 1970, as the comeback sensation petered out, RCA cashed in with *seven* album releases, including two live LPs, one Christmas record, two reissues (including the *Back in Memphis* half of *From Memphis to Vegas/From Vegas to Memphis*) and two budget label repackages. In 1975, 1976 and 1977, when Elvis was so far gone that he rarely did any studio work at all, the company still managed to crank out its contractual minimum of three albums per year.

Inevitably, such scatter-shot marketing destroyed a good deal of the renewed credibility and goodwill Elvis had created with his 1969 comeback. If a Presley album happened to coincide with a hit single or if it chronicled some event that caught the public imagination, it might do spectacularly well on the charts: *Aloha from Hawaii via Satellite*, a lackluster performance, made Number One on the charts. But Elvis' best-sellers never had much chance at chart longevity because they were too quickly succeeded by his next product. While other performers sold three, four, five, even six million copies of their LPs in the United States alone—so many records over such a long period that follow-up LPs were held back by the record label—Elvis never approached those heights. His records came and went, without impact, reaching a kind of nadir in 1972, when "Burning Love," a revived rocker that made it to Number Two on the charts, was released as part of a budget repackage, *Burning Love and Hits from His Movies, Volume 2.* For many rock fans, "Burning Love" had reestablished Elvis' mastery; the album seemed designed to belittle the single's achievement.

Yet from *On Stage—February 1970* to *Moody Blue*, released only weeks before his death in 1977, Elvis created some remarkable music. Often, he simply reworked recent hits (no matter the genre—anything from "My Way" to "Proud Mary" would do) but, from time to time, he would even stumble across a terrific original, like "Burning Love" or "I've Got a Thing About You Baby," and make it his own. He couldn't turn on the magic as effortlessly as

he had in the past—or maybe he wouldn't turn it on—but when he did, he showed more craft and as much talent as he had in the good old days. Listening to him sing Billy Swan's "I Can Help," a song originally written as an homage to Elvis, one can picture him living to a ripe old age, thriving forever on instinct and plain common sense. "Have a laugh on me, I can help," he sings. It was the closest he came to revealing his intentions.

Elvis, the greatest voice of a generation and a nation, remained a mute, struggling to his dying day to express what he had meant to say from the beginning. In his concerts the vehicles he most often used when he wanted to venture near the heart of the matter were corny but effective: "How Great Thou Art," in which he praised the Lord for all things unique, and let the implicit parallel stand for all who might see it, and "An American Trilogy," a medley devised by the country "outlaw" Mickey Newbury, which drew upon "The Battle Hymn of the Republic," "Dixie" and the spiritual "All My Trials."

Superficially, these were Elvis' attempts to sum up his achievements. If that's all one saw, then it was justifiable to find him an empty, ludicrous and sanctimonious figure. But there was a hidden motive behind those songs. Through them, Elvis was attempting to define himself and his experience according to the only standards of decent behavior he knew. And, once one perceived this motive, Elvis became something more than an arrogant clown. As he sang those maudlin verses, he became a man to pity but also an archetypal representative of the aspirations of every listener. And then the trumpet flourishes and *basso profundo* vocalizing that ended the show were not so much pretentious as they were a form of distorted beauty, like the ersatz richness of Graceland's furnishings. "An American Trilogy" might be a Naugahyde doorway, but it was the only doorway to Elvis we had.

After seeing such a performance in 1971, critic John Landau was moved to write: "Presley made greater records seventeen years ago. But in his own way he has grown as an artist.... He

Preceding pages: one of the last concerts, in Rapid City, South Dakota, June 21, 1977. Right: the cemetery after Elvis' death on August 16, 1977. Overleaf: the funeral procession through Memphis.

Mourners outside the
Graceland gates; those suffering
exhaustion were taken to aid
stations inside. Following pages:
women at Graceland, a man at
Christ Church in London. A
drunken driver plowed into the
crowd of mourners, killing two.
Bottom: one of the injured.

Amidst thousands of flowers, friends bore Elvis' coffin to the white marble mausoleum in Forest Hill Cemetery, Memphis, where he was entombed near Gladys. Overleaf: Graceland's Meditation Garden, where the graves of mother and son were moved; Vernon joined them just weeks before the second anniversary of his son's death, pictured here.

is as much a pure reflection of American popular culture as he was fifteen years ago. He is, on the one hand, gross, excessive, vain, narcissistic and violent. On the other, he is incredibly competent and professional, unpretentious, exhilaratingly visceral, innately physical and talented in the most natural and personal sense possible. He is a different artist today than he was fifteen years ago, but to me, no matter how frustrating the lapses in his career have been, he remains an artist: in fact, an American artist, and one whom we should be proud to claim as our own."

Elvis moved more than one observer to similar outbursts of complicity and generosity because he transcended himself over and over again, even after he had stopped trying. Yet it's ultimately futile to say such things. We don't know when Elvis quit on himself or even (for certain) that he did. His disappearing act was that complete. And one must wonder if it was his idea of the biggest joke of all that in his last years he finally began to sing the Chuck Berry songs that are the only ones that come close to telling his story. If Elvis hadn't been mute, then what he said would have sounded very much like Berry's "Promised Land" and "Johnny B. Goode," songs in which the singer is only a co-equal hero with the land itself, in which a rock & roll star makes the long journey from the Deep South to Hollywood, from the land of dreams and innocence to the land of guilt and reality.

Elvis never got around to singing Chuck's "Bye Bye Johnny," in which the guitar hero finally finds true love and prepares to settle down, back home, safe and free to reminisce. That was a sanctuary Elvis never reached. He wrote a different ending. It is the last genuinely majestic piece of music he recorded.

The track was cut at Graceland in February 1976, a month after Elvis turned forty-one, a year and a half before his death. The song is very simple, an old Timi Yuro ballad, "Hurt," that Elvis sings the way Jackie Wilson sang "Danny Boy," a half-dozen octaves of vocal power trying to put across a three-dimensional emotion with one-dimensional lyrics. "Hurt" makes Elvis seem a human ball of misery. And that's a lie.

You're supposed to read songs like this as the ultimate confession of how devastated Elvis was by the loss of his mother and his wife. And in turn, this sympathetic realization is supposed to excuse, or explain, his bewildering path of self-destruction.

That's nonsense. There is no explanation. And if one listens closely to songs like "Hurt," and "I Can Help," and "If I Can Dream"—if one listens clear back to "Mystery Train" and "Blue Moon"—that's what is truly heard: A voice, high and thrilled in the early days, lower and perplexed in the final months, seeking answers where there are none, clarity where there is none, cause where there is only effect.

Somewhere, out of all this, Elvis began to seem like a man who had reached some conclusions. And so he was made into a god and a king. He was neither—he was something more American and, I think, something more heroic. Elvis Presley was an explorer of vast new landscapes of dream and illusion. He was a man who refused to be told that the best of his dreams would not come true, who refused to be defined by anyone else's conceptions.

This is the goal of democracy, the journey on which every prospective American hero sets out. That Elvis made so much of the journey on his own is reason enough to remember him with the honor and love we reserve for the bravest among us. Such men made the only maps we can trust.

ELVIS
AARON
PRESLEY

JANUARY 8, 1935
AUGUST 16, 1977

SON OF
VERNON ELVIS PRESLEY
AND
GLADYS LOVE PRESLEY
FATHER OF
LISA MARIE PRESLEY

HE WAS A PRECIOUS GIFT FROM GOD
HE CHERISHED AND LOVED DEARLY.

HE HAD A GOD-GIVEN TALENT THAT HE SHARED
WITH THE WORLD. AND WITHOUT A DOUBT.
HE BECAME MOST WIDELY ACCLAIMED:
CAPTURING THE HEARTS OF YOUNG AND OLD ALIKE.

HE WAS ADMIRED NOT ONLY AS AN ENTERTAINER.
BUT AS THE GREAT HUMANITARIAN THAT HE WAS:
FOR HIS GENEROSITY, AND HIS KIND FEELINGS
FOR HIS FELLOW MAN.

HE REVOLUTIONIZED THE FIELD OF MUSIC AND
RECEIVED ITS HIGHEST AWARDS.

HE BECAME A LIVING LEGEND IN HIS OWN TIME.
EARNING THE RESPECT AND LOVE OF MILLIONS.

GOD SAW THAT HE NEEDED SOME REST AND
CALLED HIM HOME TO BE WITH HIM.

WE MISS YOU. SON AND DADDY. I THANK GOD
THAT HE GAVE US YOU AS OUR SON.

BY VERNON PRESLEY

lvis World"
R.D. 388 BOUNDBROOK N.J. 08805.

ELVIS PRESLEY TRIB

DISCOGRAPHY

This listing of more than 150 Elvis Presley recordings is organized chronologically by year of recording (rather than by type of music, year of release or appearance on LPs) for a number of reasons. Elvis' catalogue is a complete jumble; there is no single collection of his best music. (*The Sun Sessions*; *Worldwide 50 Gold Award Hits, Volume One*; the four *Golden Hits* collections; the TV-special soundtrack and *From Elvis in Memphis* barely scratch the surface.) This is understandable, given the artistic neglect that surrounded Elvis at RCA. The predictable result is that Elvis' music must be taken piecemeal to be understood. (In three cases below, entire concerts are recommended, but these are pure anomalies.)

This is a discography then of Elvis' best recordings. The selections leave out nothing indispensable, and include little that's marginal. Their diversity—"Hound Dog" giving way to "Bosom of Abraham" yielding to "An American Trilogy"—is proof enough of Presley's artistic scope. By making the organization purely chronological, I hoped to establish also the continuity of Elvis' career, to prove once and for all that he was not a great singer for one or two isolated years but for two decades almost continuously. Doubters are advised to listen to the evidence. Defense rests.

1954

"Blue Moon"
"Blue Moon of Kentucky"
"Good Rockin' Tonight"
"Milkcow Blues Boogie"
"That's All Right"
"Trying to Get to You"

1955

"Baby, Let's Play House"
"I'm Left, You're Right, She's Gone"
"Mystery Train"
"You're a Heartbreaker"

These ten songs are the best of the tracks Elvis recorded for Sam Phillips at Sun Records in Memphis. They are all contained on the RCA album *The Sun Sessions*, which is highly recommended.

1956

"Any Way You Want Me (That's How I Will Be)"
"Blue Suede Shoes"*
"Don't Be Cruel"
"Flip Flop and Fly"**
"Heartbreak Hotel"
"Hound Dog"
"I Got a Woman"
"I Want You, I Need You, I Love You"
"I Was the One"
"Lawdy Miss Clawdy"
"Love Me"

"Love Me Tender"
"Money Honey"
"My Baby Left Me"
"Paralyzed"
"Reddy Teddy"
"Rip It Up"
"Shake Rattle and Roll"**
"Too Much"
"We're Gonna Move"
"When My Blue Moon Turns to Gold Again"

*Elvis recorded a markedly inferior version of this song for the soundtrack of *G.I. Blues*. The version recommended is contained on the album *Elvis Presley* (with the pink-and-green cover).

**Soundtrack recordings from the Dorsey Brothers TV show. These are contained on the soundtrack album to *This Is Elvis*. The version of "Shake Rattle and Roll" contained on *For LP Fans Only* is much inferior.

As if Elvis hadn't been sufficiently prolific during 1956, on December 4, he dropped by Sun Records to pay a social call. Carl Perkins was engaged in the session that produced his hit "Matchbox," and Johnny Cash and Jerry Lee Lewis were also around. Soon, the four gathered round the piano to sing hymns, current hits and whatever came to mind—a session long rumored to exist as an "underground" tape known as the Million Dollar Quartet. In 1981, the tape surfaced as an album— pressed with dubious legality and not easy to find, but pressed nonetheless. Apparently, the two sides contained on *The Million Dollar Quartet* (OMD 001) are but a fragment of the material actually taped by Sun engineer Jack Clement, but a remarkable fragment it is—about forty minutes of gospel harmonizing on tunes ranging from "Down by the Riverside" and "Peace in the Valley" to "Farther Along" and a Pat Boone hit Elvis claimed to have rejected, "I'm with the Crowd But Oh So Alone." *The Million Dollar Quartet* is well worth seeking out for anyone interested in hearing Elvis singing spontaneously and at ease, for those fascinated in the roots of Presley and of rockabilly and for anyone who doubts Elvis' complete command of all musical situations. This material is hardly as revelatory as Presley's official recordings of the period, but its homely honesty makes it mesmerizing.

1957

"All Shook Up"
"(You're So Square) Baby, I Don't Care"
"Blueberry Hill"
"Don't"
"Don't Leave Me Now"
"Got a Lot o' Livin' to Do"
"I Beg of You"
"I Want to Be Free"
"It Is No Secret"
"Jailhouse Rock"
"Loving You"
"Mean Woman Blues"

"One Night"
"Peace in the Valley"
"Take My Hand, Precious Lord"
"(Let Me Be Your) Teddy Bear"
"Treat Me Nice"
"When It Rains, It Really Pours"*
"Young and Beautiful"

*Although this performance of the blues originally recorded by Billy "The Kid" Emerson for Sun ranks with Elvis' best pure blues singing ever, it was mysteriously not released until the 1965 album, *Elvis for Everyone*.

1958

"A Big Hunk o' Love"
"Blue Christmas"
"Crawfish"
"Danny"
"Hard Headed Woman"
"I Need Your Love Tonight"
"King Creole"
"My Wish Came True"
"Santa Claus Is Back in Town"
"Trouble"
"Wear My Ring around Your Neck"

1959

No recording. In military service in West Germany.

1960

"Ain't That Loving You Baby"
"Are You Lonesome Tonight?"
"Fame and Fortune"
"A Fool Such As I"
"G.I. Blues"
"His Hand in Mine"
"It's Now or Never"
"Joshua Fit the Battle"
"Reconsider Baby"
"Stuck on You"
"Such a Night"
"Swing Down, Sweet Chariot"
"Working on the Building"

1961

"Blue Hawaii"
"Can't Help Falling in Love with You"
"Crying in the Chapel"*
"Follow That Dream"
"Good Luck Charm"
"(Marie's the Name) His Latest Flame"
"I Feel So Bad"
"Little Sister"

*Although "Crying in the Chapel" was recorded at the sessions for the *His Hand in Mine* album (from which the other spirituals and hymns listed here are drawn), and although "Crying" was undoubtedly the stellar performance of that session, it was not released until 1965.

1962

"King of the Whole Wide World"
"Return to Sender"
"She's Not You"
"Suspicion"

239

1963

"C'mon Everybody"
"(You're the) Devil in Disguise"
"One Broken Heart for Sale"
"Please Don't Drag That String Around"
"Viva Las Vegas"
"What'd I Say"

1964

"It Hurts Me"
"Little Egypt"
"Memphis, Tennessee"

1965

A complete washout; no convenient military excuses.

1966

"Down in the Valley"
"How Great Thou Art"
"If Everyday Was Like Christmas"
"I'll Be Back"
"Long Legged Girl (with the Short Dress On)"
"Spinout"
"Stand by Me"
"Stop Look and Listen"
"Tomorrow Is a Long Time"
"Where Could I Go But to the Lord?"

1967

"Big Boss Man"
"Guitar Man"
"Hi-Heel Sneakers"
"Let Yourself Go"
"You Don't Know Me"

1968

"Baby, What You Want Me to Do?"
"Blue Christmas"
"Can't Help Falling in Love"
"If I Can Dream"
"Lawdy, Miss Clawdy"
"One Night"
"Too Much Monkey Business"
"Trouble/Guitar Man"
"U.S. Male"
"Where Could I Go But to the Lord?"

Note: With the exception of "Too Much Monkey Business" and "U.S. Male," all of the music above appears in the *Elvis TV Special* album (RCA LPM 4088). This music represents a radical departure from the pap Elvis had been recording, of course, but it also represents a maturing of all the tendencies in the music listed above it. A further exploration of this new form of Elvis' singing (and, amazingly enough, guitar playing) can be heard on the bootleg album *The Burbank Sessions, Vol. 1,* one of the greatest concert recordings ever made. The live tracks from the TV special only hint at what's here.

1969

"After Loving You"
"Any Day Now"

"I'm Movin' On"
"In the Ghetto"
"It Keeps Right On A-Hurtin' "
"Kentucky Rain"
"Long Black Limousine"
"Only the Strong Survive"
"Stranger in My Own Home Town"
"Suspicious Minds"
"Wearin' That Loved On Look"
"Without Love (There Is Nothing)"

These are, of course, the famous Chips Moman-produced sessions from American Recording Studios in Memphis, with the backing band led by Tommy Cogbill. In addition, the two live recordings Elvis did in Las Vegas during this period should be heard. The first—*Elvis in Person at the International Hotel in Las Vegas*—was recorded during his first stint there and represents his breakthrough in live performance. By the time of *On Stage—February 1970,* Elvis had almost, but not quite, settled into a full exposition of the ritual discussed in chapter ten. What saves him is the musical vogue of the time, a direct descendant of rockabilly called "swamp rock," which was popularized by Creedence Clearwater Revival and Tony Joe White. *On Stage* is the apotheosis of swamp rock and proof of how creative Elvis could be even within the limitations of a Vegas set. Like *The Burbank Sessions* bootleg, these live recordings need to be heard on their own; while there are outstanding individual tracks, the continuity of the performance tells a larger, more important story, something that is true of few (perhaps no) other Elvis albums.

1970

"Bridge over Troubled Water"*
"Got My Mojo Workin' "
"I Was Born About 10,000 Years Ago"
"I Washed My Hands in Muddy Water"
"It's Your Baby, You Rock It"
"Make the World Go Away"
"Snowbird"

*Although "Bridge over Troubled Water" is presented as a live track on the documentary-movie soundtrack album *That's The Way It Is,* this is almost surely a studio recording with overdubbed applause—something noteworthy only because Elvis cheated so rarely, others (in this regard) so often.

1971

"Amazing Grace"
"Bosom of Abraham"
"Don't Think Twice . . . It's Alright"
"Early Morning Rain"
"For Lovin' Me"
"He Touched Me"
"If I Get Home on Christmas Day"
"I'll Be Home on Christmas Day"
"Merry Christmas Baby"
"Put Your Hand in the Hand"

1972

"An American Trilogy"*

"Burning Love"

*Recorded live at Madison Square Garden: This is the first recording Elvis made of the song. In most other respects, the hastily mixed and basically unedited Madison Square Garden live album is weak and uninteresting.

1973

"Are You Sincere?"
"Good Time Charlie's Got the Blues"
"I've Got a Thing About You Baby"
"Johnny B. Goode"*
"My Boy"
"Promised Land"
"Raised on Rock"
"Steamroller Blues"*
"You Gave Me a Mountain"*

*These are from the soundtrack to Elvis' television special *Aloha from Hawaii—Via Satellite.* In many respects, the quality of the performances on "Johnny B. Goode" and "You Gave Me a Mountain" is secondary to the fact that Elvis now performed such seemingly autobiographical material boldly and with a straight face. "Steamroller Blues" is just about the only outstanding performance from an otherwise lackluster media "event."

1974

Elvis' only recording activity in this year was a March 20 concert in Memphis, released as a live album later that year. The record produced two minor hit singles, "Steamroller Blues" and "An American Trilogy" but, despite these, and the fact that *Elvis as Recorded Live on Stage in Memphis* is meant to be a "homecoming" show, a third "concert event" LP (along with the Madison Square Garden and Aloha shows), it is just as mediocre as Presley's other mid-Seventies concert records.

1975

"Green Green Grass of Home"
"I Can Help"
"Shake a Hand"

1976

"Hurt"
"Moody Blue"
"Pledging My Love"
"She Thinks I Still Care"
"Way Down"

All of these were recorded at Graceland, Elvis being too ill to attend a recording-studio session, even if he had been willing to do so (which he probably was not).

1977

Elvis made no studio recordings at all and no live recordings of intrinsic merit in the last year of his life. But he left behind a final revelatory performance: The slobbering, hapless rendition of "Are You Lonesome Tonight?" which is contained in the film

This Is Elvis and included, warts and all, on the soundtrack album to that film and on *Elvis in Concert*, the soundtrack to the CBS television special shown shortly after his death. This version of "Are You Lonesome Tonight?" tells most interested Elvis observers all they need to know—and more than many want to find out—about his condition at the time of his death. He did not die of a heart attack.

FILMOGRAPHY

Love Me Tender (Twentieth Century-Fox), November 1956. Directed by Robert D. Webb; with Deborah Paget.

Loving You (Paramount), released July 1957; directed by Hal Kantor; with Lizabeth Scott, Wendell Corey and Dolores Hart.

Jailhouse Rock (MGM), October 1957. Directed by Richard Thorpe; with Mickey Shaughnessy, Judy Tyler, Dean Jones and Vaughn Taylor.

King Creole (Paramount), May 1958. Directed by Michael Curtiz; with Carolyn Jones, Dolores Hart, Dean Jagger and Walter Matthau.

G.I. Blues (Paramount), October 1960. Directed by Norman Taurog; with Juliet Prowse.

Flaming Star (Twentieth Century-Fox), December 1960. Directed by Don Siegel; with Barbara Eden, Steve Forrest, John McIntire and Delores Del Rio.

Wild in the Country (Twentieth Century-Fox), June 1961. Directed by Philip Dunne; with Hope Lange, John Ireland, Tuesday Weld and Gary Lockwood.

Blue Hawaii (Paramount), November 1961. Directed by Norman Taurog; with Angela Lansbury, Joan Blackman and Iris Adrian.

Follow That Dream (United Artists), March 1962. Directed by Gordon Douglas; with Arthur O'Connell, Joanna Moore and Ann Helm.

Kid Galahad (United Artists), July 1962. Directed by Phil Karlson; with Gig Young, Lola Albright, Charles Bronson and Joan Blackman.

Girls! Girls! Girls! (Paramount), November 1962. Directed by Norman Taurog; with Stella Stevens and Jeremy Slate.

It Happened at the World's Fair (MGM), April 1963. Directed by Norman Taurog; with Joan O'Brien, Gary Lockwood and Yvonne Craig.

Fun in Acapulco (Paramount), November 1963. Directed by Richard Thorpe; with Ursula Andress, Paul Lukas and Alejandro Ray.

Kissin' Cousins (MGM), March 1964. Directed by Gene Nelson; with Pamela Astin, Yvonne Craig and Arthur O'Connell.

Viva Las Vegas (MGM), April 1964. Directed by George Sidney; with Ann-Margret, Cesare Denova and William Demarest.

Roustabout (Paramount), November 1964. Directed by John Rich; with Barbara Stanwyck, Joan Freeman and Sue Ann Langdon.

Girl Happy (MGM), January 1965. Directed by Boris Sagal; with Shelley Fabares, Mary Ann Mobley, Chris Noel and Joby Baker.

Tickle Me (Allied Artists), June 1965. Directed by Norman Taurog; with Jocelyn Lane, Julie Adams and Jack Mullaney.

Harum Scarum (MGM), December 1965. Directed by Gene Nelson; with Mary Ann Mobley and Fran Jeffries.

Paradise, Hawaiian Style (Paramount), June 1966. Directed by Michael Moore; with Suzanna Leigh, James Shigeta and Donna Butterworth.

Frankie and Johnny (United Artists), July 1966. Directed by Frederick De Cordova; with Donna Douglas, Harry Morgan and Sue Ann Langdon.

Spinout (MGM), December 1966. Directed by Norman Taurog; with Deborah Walley and Shelley Fabares.

Double Trouble (MGM), May 1967. Directed by Norman Taurog; with Annette Day, John Williams, the Wiere Brothers.

Easy Come, Easy Go (Paramount), June 1967. Directed by John Rich; with Elsa Lanchester, Pat Priest and Dodi Marshal.

Clambake (United Artists), December 1967. Directed by Arthur H. Nadel; with Shelley Fabares and Bill Bixby.

Stay Away, Joe (MGM), March 1968. Directed by Peter Tewksbury; with Burgess Meredith, Joan Blondell and L. Q. Jones.

Speedway (MGM), June 1968. Directed by Norman Taurog; with Nancy Sinatra, Bill Bixby and Gale Gordon.

Live a Little, Love a Little (MGM), October 1968. Directed by Norman Taurog; with Rudy Vallee, Eddie Hodges and Michele Carey.

Charro! (National General Productions Inc.), September 1969. Directed by Charles Marquis Warren; with Lynn Kellogg.

The Trouble with Girls (And How to Get into It) (MGM), December 1969. Directed by Peter Tewksbury; with Sheree North, Vincent Price and John Carradine.

Change of Habit (NBC-Universal), January 1970. Directed by William Graham; with Mary Tyler Moore.

Elvis: That's the Way It Is (MGM), December 1970. Directed by Denis Sanders.

Elvis on Tour (MGM), 1972. Directed by Pierre Adidge and Robert Abel.

BIBLIOGRAPHY

Taken together, these books and articles form an index of what I've referred to as "the Elvis myth," various and contradictory as it often is. Since it is intended not only as a catalogue of my sources and influences but also as a reading list for the Elvis-obsessed, I've included explanatory notes with each entry.

Cash, W. J. *The Mind of the South*. New York: Vintage, 1941; New York: Knopf, 1960. Every writer about Elvis and/or rockabilly returns to Cash's definitive descriptions of the hillbilly milieu, but, mostly, they get it wrong: What's most applicable to Elvis here isn't Cash's description of how the feudalism of the South holds men bound, but his analysis of how difficult it is for a man to truly break free of those restrictions. A classic study of Americans in America; one's major regret is that Cash did not live to reassess Southerners in light of Elvis and rockabilly.

Cortez, Diego, ed. *Private Elvis*. Stuttgart, W. Germany: Fey, 1978. Probably the weirdest Elvis book; possibly the strangest Elvis artifact. In the early pages, Cortez and his colleague, Duncan Smith, engage in a heavily semiotic analysis of Elvis' relationship to his image. This is followed by the photographs of Rudolf Paulini, which are the most surreal examples of that relationship ever publicly shown. For the most part, they are shots of Elvis with various West German hookers and B-girls, some of them lovely, many of them grotesque. Elvis displays a bewildering variety of expressions, each of them opaque, but the photos remain revealing since they force one to imagine Elvis' response to their existence: Had they been published while he was still in the Army (or even later), they might have ruined him. A bit creepy, never rising above the sordid, these pictures are like the answer to a question no

241

one thought to ask: What do Elvis and Philip Marlowe have in common?

Crumbaker, Marge, and Tucker, Gabe. *Up and Down with Elvis: The Inside Story.* New York: Putnam, 1981. Crumbaker is a Houston newspaper columnist, but this is Tucker's story. He's a Col. Parker crony and, of course, this is a version of the tale in which the Colonel represents genius at its purest while Elvis is a mere window shade, to be drawn at will. Tucker never reveals much, probably because he was an arm's-length insider: He did Parker's press-relations work, which may make him the Ronald Ziegler of rock & roll. Yet Tucker was around for enough interesting goings on to provide some suggestions about the real motivations of Parker's often murky associations with RCA and Hill and Range.

Farren, Mick, and Marchbank, Pearce. *Elvis in His Own Words.* New York: Omnibus Press, 1977. Elvis quotes from all ages, none of them identified as to source or context, which makes the book useless to unreliable as a reference. But it is a particularly unsubtle extension of the theory that Elvis was the product of luck more than talent. And all those unsourced quotes, festering in their clichés, go a long way toward making the case that he was indeed a public mute.

Flippo, Chet. *Your Cheatin' Heart: A Biography of Hank Williams.* New York: Simon and Schuster, 1981. A gloves-off account of his life, which has certain connections to Elvis', though they are more linked to drugs than music. Flippo is indispensable for his analysis of the nature of the country-music audience, its loyalties and expectations, which were tremendously important in shaping Elvis' career.

Gillett, Charlie. *The Sound of the City: The Rise of Rock and Roll.* New York: Outerbridge and Dienstfrey, 1970. A purist's history of rock's first decade or so. Gillett believes that Elvis' ruination was in being signed to RCA: "rock'n'roll off the production line," he calls everything from "Heartbreak Hotel" onward. Unfortunately, this argument is peripheral to the book's main concern and is never fully developed there. However, Gillett's allusions to Elvis' total failure at RCA are indicative of the purist attitude, which finds its most complete and interesting expression in Peter Guralnick's writing (*see below*).

Goldman, Albert. *Elvis.* New York: McGraw-Hill, 1981. Overwritten, bloated fantasy/biography written by the journalistic graverobber of Lenny Bruce. Goldman loathes rock & roll, Southerners, the poor—almost everything Elvis represented in American culture. These attitudes aren't surprising, coming from a defrocked academic; more disturbing is

the vengeance with which Goldman attempts to complete the job begun by Steve Allen, the CBS censors, Hal Wallis, Col. Parker and Hill and Range. Thanks to the aid of the traitorous Memphis Mafioso Lamar Fike, Goldman comes very near to actually casting a pall over Elvis' life. Fortunately, he screws up, first by hyping all of his information into unbelievable proportions of "revelation"; second, by failing to cite his sources, so that every fact is of doubtful veracity; finally, by alleging that Elvis couldn't sing—a charge so ludicrous that only a sycophant could emerge from this work with a shred of respect left for its author.

Gregory, Neal and Janice. *When Elvis Died.* Washington, D. C.: Communications Press, 1980; New York: Pocket, 1982. Scrupulously researched description and analysis of media reaction to the news of Elvis' death and the ensuing national and international trauma. The Gregorys are interested primarily in the media, second in Elvis as an archetypal Southerner, not very much at all in Elvis as a singer and are barely aware that he was an important artist. Yet their reportage is a yeoman's job that simply blows away most of the fluff and puffery that's been published about Elvis since he died.

Guralnick, Peter. *Lost Highway.* Boston: Godine, 1979. Guralnick offers the urmyth for purists—a view of Elvis so pristine that at one point he actually comments: ". . . if Elvis Presley had simply disappeared after leaving the little Sun studio for the last time, his status would be something like that of a latter-day Robert Johnson: lost, vulnerable, eternally youthful, forever on the edge, pure and timeless." It's hard not to feel that Guralnick wishes this had happened, that he would rather not have to deal with what came after. But Guralnick does deal with it and, though his hostility to success in general strikes me as pecksniffian, there's no denying that he wrestles with the myth as ably as anyone. There are two essays about Elvis in this volume: The first, a critical/biographical sketch, also appears in *The Rolling Stone Illustrated History of Rock & Roll*; the second is a kind of belated obituary. Both are loving, concerned, moving, infected with the generosity of spirit that is characteristic of the Sun sides themselves. Guralnick closes his book (a series of profiles of blues, R&B and C&W musicians) with a lengthy profile/interview with Sam Phillips, which is simultaneously the best thing ever written about Phillips and by far the most credulous. Taken with a healthy dose of salt, however, even this is worthwhile.

Hawkins, Martin, and Escott, Colin. *Catalyst: The Sun Records Story.* New York: Aquarius Books, 1975. Largely the gospel according to Sam Phillips but also a really thorough, accurate survey of all the

music made at Sun. Bedrock legend-making here; no revelations but indispensable for getting the facts squared away, not only about Elvis but about the rockabillies who followed him (and the bluesmen who preceded him).

Hawkins, Martin, and Escott, Colin. *Elvis: The Illustrated Discography.* London: Omnibus, 1981. This discography, originally published in 1974 (as *The Elvis Session File: 20 Years of Elvis*) obviously can add very little in the way of fact to the Jorgenson and Matthew-Walker discographies (*see below*). But even though the musicology isn't as astute as Matthew-Walker's, Hawkins and Escott are a lot better organized—and the typographic design of the book makes cross-referencing individual tracks and albums one hell of a lot easier. It ought to go without saying that such cross-referencing is the essence of Elvis-watching. This book also has the most comprehensive bootleg listing I know of.

Hopkins, Jerry. *Elvis: A Biography.* New York: Simon and Schuster, 1971.

Hopkins, Jerry. *Elvis: The Final Years.* New York: St. Martin's Press, 1980. The only rock biography with a sequel. Even (perhaps that ought to be especially) after Goldman, Hopkins remains the best source for a basic factual Presley bio. It has been said that these books contain no analysis, but that's not strictly true. As becomes unavoidably clear in the second volume, Hopkins considers Elvis' success primarily the product of Col. Parker's shrewdness. Consider this, then, the closest we have to an "official" view of Elvis.

Jorgenson, Ernst; Rasmussen, Erik; and Mikkelson, Johnny. *Elvis Recording Sessions.* Stenløse, Denmark: JEE-production, 1977. A complete listing by date of all Elvis sessions, including musicians present, tracks recorded and sundry supplemental facts. Not as valuable for its commentary as the Matthew-Walker discography, but stronger on facts.

Lacker, Marty and Patsy; and Smith, Leslie. *Elvis: Portrait of a Friend.* New York: Bantam, 1979. Though this is one of the more coherent confessions of the Memphis Mafia, it is also utterly typical in its attempt to convey a two-part message: 1) *We were there and this is the truth;* 2) *It wasn't our fault.* Neither part is totally convincing.

Landau, Jon. *It's Too Late to Stop Now.* San Francisco: Straight Arrow, 1972. Landau's review of a 1971 Elvis show in Boston, "In Praise of Elvis Presley," remains the most generous appraisal of Elvis' postcomeback stage shows because Landau is the only critic who not only understands but *accepts* that Elvis no longer is (and no longer wishes to be) a rock & roll star. And in this matter, acceptance is the essence.

Lichter, Paul. *The Boy Who Dared to Rock: The Definitive Elvis*. New York: Doubleday, 1978. This collection of dull and transparent trivia is devoted to the Elvis-as-godhead school of thought which figures since Lichter makes his (considerable) wages as the world's leading purveyor of Elvis merchandise. Lichter's love for Presley is unquestionable—without it, he could never have trivialized him so well or nearly as completely. This book is useful only if you need perspective desperately or if you're contemplating a career as an Elvis impersonator and would like a wardrobe catalogue.

Mann, May. *The Private Elvis*. New York: Pocket, 1977. Mann is a writer for fan magazines of the glossy, newsstand sort and her account contains nothing that would make readers of the *Photoplay* genre blush. She once kissed Elvis (it was all part of the interview), she believes Col. Parker is a genius and she all but denies that Elvis could possibly have taken drugs, or done anything else to excess. Saturday-morning cartoon shows are more credible.

Marcus, Greil. *Mystery Train: Images of America in Rock 'n' Roll Music*. New York: E. P. Dutton, 1975. Marcus' "Presliad," the 15,000-word concluding section of this book, is as close to a critical summation as anyone has come in writing about the earliest days of Elvis' career, and it's unlikely that anyone will ever write better about the Sun recordings themselves. And Marcus has a deep understanding both of what drove Elvis and of what attracted us to him. Although Marcus is far too dismissive of the middle years of Presley's career, it remains impossible to discuss Elvis seriously as an artist without referring frequently to the work done here. Indeed, before the publication of *Mystery Train*, it was all but impossible to discuss Elvis, period. A great book on America, popular music and their interaction.

Matthew-Walker, Robert. *Elvis Presley: A Study in Music*. Tunbridge Wells, Kent, England: Midas Books, 1979. Talk about thankless tasks. Matthew-Walker here evaluates every officially released song in the Presley catalogue. Although his judgments aren't necessarily mine (I'm not a big fan of "Please Don't Drag That String Around," much less "Just Tell Her Jim Said Hello"), Matthew-Walker makes wading through the thicket of Presley's musical trivia much easier.

Palmer, Robert. *Deep Blues*. New York: Viking, 1981. For its serious, if brief, discussion of Elvis within the strict limits of the blues tradition.

Presley, Dee; Stanley, Bill, Rick and David (as told to Martin Torgoff). *Elvis, We Loved You Tender*. New York: Delacorte, 1980. Another insider chronicle from the Memphis Mafiosi—these related by marriage (Dee was Vernon's second wife, the Stanley boys thus Elvis' step-brothers). It wasn't their fault, either.

Presley, Vester, and Rooks, Nancy. *The Presley Family Cookbook*. Memphis, Tenn.: Wimmer Brothers Books, 1980. Are these the real culprits? Well, the peanut butter sandwich recipe calls for one-quarter of a cup of margarine, melted, and there's always the low-calorie Pepsi-Cola salad, not to mention baked ham with beer. This is actually a fairly interesting Southern cookbook, if what you want is an example of how people really cook in Memphis as opposed to recipes that encourage gourmandising.

Stearn, Jess, with Geller, Larry. *The Truth About Elvis*. New York: Jove, 1980. If Elvis was muddled in his religious beliefs, no wonder. Geller is another Presley minion (he never spent much time in Memphis, being an L.A. hairdresser when they met, which presumably excludes him from the Mafiosi proper—though it wasn't his fault, either), whose principal task seems to have been keeping the King current with the latest in mysticism. This fed Presley's megalomaniacal tendency to regard himself as a saint or a messiah—Stearn and Geller also seem to be convinced that Elvis approached godliness—or would have done, if only he'd listened to Larry (not to be confused with Uri). Possibly the funniest book here.

Tharpe, Jac L., ed. *Elvis: Images and Fancies*. Jackson, Miss.: University Press of Mississippi, 1981. These are academic essays for the most part, but, perhaps in tribute to the incessantly interesting subject, they're some of the most vital, least dry-boned academic essays ever written. Although even the best of them is occasionally overwhelmed by Southern provincialism (Elvis was *not* a Southerner first though he was a Southerner even when he wasn't anything else), Linda Ray Pratt and Van K. Brock, among others, have rethought Elvis and his music in provocative new ways. The work here is fundamental and long overdue and deserves the widest possible audience. It blows some cobwebs off the more hackneyed parts of Elvis mythology, adds some interesting new branches for further speculation and is relentless in its insistence upon Presley's significance, not only as an American totem but as an American artist.

Wertheimer, Alfred. *Elvis '56: In the Beginning*. New York: Collier, 1979. In 1956, Wertheimer was hired by RCA Records to shoot some pictures at Elvis' first New York recording session (which produced "Hound Dog" and "Don't Be Cruel"). In the end, he also journeyed with Elvis, the Colonel and entourage by train to Memphis and then over to a Fourth of July concert Elvis gave in a park. The photos that comprise this volume—the text, very brief, is Wertheimer's reminiscence of the circumstances—are a revelation: The shots of Elvis and Gladys, in particular, add an eerie sidelight to their relationship. Not only did he and Priscilla look alike—so did he and his mother. And their closeness is complete; he changes clothes in her presence, which is fairly remarkable for a twenty-one-year-old. On the other hand, there is a certain joyous innocence that Wertheimer has also caught—Elvis, French kissing a groupie in a stairwell backstage or sitting at a soda fountain, waiting for his train, is still a kid trying to get a hold on his manhood. Rare and priceless portraits.

West, Red and Sonny; Hebler, Dave; as told to Steve Dunleavy. *Elvis: What Happened?* New York: Ballantine, 1977. The original "don't blame it on me" tome, in which three disenfranchised Mafiosi blow the whistle on Elvis' more peculiar habits regarding drugs and violence. Not exactly an authoritative source—even the Wests seemed upset with how much Dunleavy's yellow journalism distorted the facts—but undeniably powerful, especially since this book was published only days before Elvis (who knew what it would reveal) died. In the end, no one has done a scandal book on Elvis that supersedes this one.

Willis, Ellen. *Beginning to See the Light*. New York: Knopf, 1981. Willis' *New Yorker* review of Presley's first appearance in Vegas in 1968, though steeped in hippie rhetoric about both Elvis and Vegas, remains the best account.

Worth, Fred L., and Tamerius, Steve D. *All About Elvis*. New York: Bantam, 1981. An exhaustive compilation of 400 pages of Elvis trivia, including some startling facts, albeit most of them minor. That is, I love knowing the name of the guy Elvis' mother bought his first guitar from, but I wish the book were sufficiently well-organized to let me locate this little gem once again. The discographical information includes a listing of each song Elvis recorded, the albums and singles on which they appear, names of the composers, and notes important earlier versions, which makes this a necessary complement to the Matthew-Walker and Jorgenson-Rasmussen-Mikkelson discographies.

Note: All chart positions referred to in the text are based on Joel Whitburn's *Record Research*, which compiles *Billboard* chart information of the rock & roll era.

CREDITS